CHASE THE ROAR

Becoming Faith Chasers in an American Dream Culture

ARIEL TYSON

Copyright © 2017 Ariel Tyson

All rights reserved. No part of this publication may be reproduced, distributed, or transmitted in any form or by any means, including photocopying, recording, or other electronic or mechanical methods, without the prior written permission of the publisher, except in the case of brief quotations embodied in reviews and certain other non-commercial uses permitted by copyright law.

Unless otherwise indicated, Scripture quotations are from the Holy Bible, New International Version®. NIV®. Copyright © 1973, 1978, 1984, 2011 by Biblical, Inc.™

Scripture quotations labeled EXB are from the Holy Bible, The Expanded Bible® (EXB®), Copyright © 2011 by Thomas Nelson, Inc. All rights reserved.

Scripture quotations labeled NKJV are from the Holy Bible, The New King James Version® (NKJV®), Copyright © 1982 by Thomas Nelson, Inc. All rights reserved.

Scripture quotations labeled ESV are from The Holy Bible, English Standard Version® (ESV®) Permanent Text Edition® (2016), Copyright © 2001 by Crossway Bibles, a publishing ministry of Good News Publishers. All rights reserved.

Cover Design: Les Solot

PRAISE FOR *CHASE THE ROAR*

This book contains practical steps for living a life of faith, conveyed in an engaging, real-life story. Ariel Tyson, her husband, and their young, growing family are living and learning what the true "American Dream" is all about, and it is very different than the perception the world portrays.

—**Dr. Bill Agee**, Executive Director, California Southern Baptist Convention

Ariel offers a fresh and honest look at how her faith is the cornerstone of her life. This is a great read for people of all ages. I have known Ariel for many years and am inspired by these pages!

—**Megan Alexander**, reporter for *Inside Edition* and author of *Faith in the Spotlight*

Ariel has a wonderful way of telling a story from the genuine places of her life and of weaving incredible truth and encouragement from God's Word. This book was an encouragement to me, and I know it will be to others as well.

—**Brittany Price Brooker**, speaker, blogger, and artist BrittanyPrice.com

What I appreciate most from Ariel Tyson's courageous book is that she places living a life of faith for Christ as the preeminent charge to all believers; but especially to young people, who are faced with so much challenge and temptation to compromise and pursue earthier goals. It has been said by many wise men and women that success begins and ends with pursuing a vision much greater than ourselves. Jesus said it this way: "Greater love has no one than this, than to lay one's life down for his friends" (John 15:13, NKJV). This important book asks each true follower of our Lord to do just that: put all things after serving God first. All things. So I do give this important, heartfelt work my high commendation to all Christian readers who wish to be true disciples of the Master, and nothing less.

—**Dr. Cliff Kelly**, professor, speaker, and author of *The Sixth Seal*

Ariel's bold faith is riveting. Want to know how to live life as a passionate pursuit? Ariel leaves no question unanswered as she draws a line right through the temptation to live by other's standards.

—**Brooke Sailer**, author of *This Thing Called Home*

Having worked with ministers' wives for many years, I have a special place in my heart for young church planters' wives. We call them church planters' wives, but in reality, they are much more. They are partners in ministry: wives, mothers, teachers, leaders, daughters, friends, mentors, and much more. The demands and expectations of this life of faith, whether from others or self-imposed, can be overwhelming. Ariel has shared the story of how God has worked in her heart to change her goal from chasing after the "American Dream" to chasing after God's Plan. And as she says in her book, "God's adventures are the best adventures."

—**Pam Agee**, mentor and prayer partner to church planting wives

This book is dedicated to those who believed in this dream.

My husband, Michael – for pushing me to step out in faith and allow God to use me in this way. You have always believed in me and encouraged me in everything I do. I would have never completed this book if it wasn't for you. I love you more each day.

My children – for bearing with me and understanding the bigger picture, and for being my daily inspiration to continue modeling a life of faith.

My parents – for your deep love and showing me where hard work and determination can take me and for always believing that I could accomplish all of my dreams.

My in-laws – for raising my best friend and welcoming me into your family with so much love, without whom I wouldn't have these specific faith opportunities.

And the rest of my dear family and friends – for your love and encouraging me throughout the entire book-writing process!

TABLE OF CONTENTS

Foreword	*1*
Introduction	*3*
Part One: Exchanging Dreams	**9**
Chapter One: Anchor in a Raging Sea	*11*
Chapter Two: The Bare Necessities	*17*
Chapter Three: A Giant Leap	*23*
Chapter Four: Homesick	*29*
Part Two: The Chase	**37**
Chapter Five: Plankton and the Ocean Current	*39*
Chapter Six: Chase the Roar	*51*
Chapter Seven: All Your Might	*61*
Chapter Eight: Big Faith, Bigger God	*91*
Chapter Nine: Lions for Jesus	*117*
Chapter Ten: Put Your Money Where Your Mouth Is	*127*
Chapter Eleven: Prepared Heroes Move the World	*143*
Chapter Twelve: Cause the Ripple	*155*
Epilogue	*167*
Acknowledgments	*171*
Notes	*173*
Spiritual Gifts Survey	*177*
The Faith Challenge	*187*
About The Author	*189*

FOREWORD

I HAVE BEEN AN ADVOCATE for freedom through faith in Jesus since the first day I began following him in 1973. My entire life and ministry has involved walking by faith, even when the future is unknown. In my early days of ministry, there were countless men and women of God who blessed my wife, Janet, and me as we pursued God's calling on our lives. These men and women of faith inspired us to continue our pursuit of making big faith decisions, following the call of God on our lives, being leaders in this field, and learning how to generously give with a humble heart. These are all values I have shared with Ariel and her husband, Michael, throughout our mentoring relationship as they've navigated their faith life and the early days of ministry.

Ariel's faith journey has been a main contributor to why she is the pastor's wife, leader, encourager, counselor, mother, and friend that she is today. Her faith journey has spanned the entirety of her 18-year walk with Christ and, even as a young child, she observed the faith walks of loved ones in her life. I have witnessed Ariel and Michael affect change in the lives of people in their community, country, and across the world by living out their testimony by taking both the small and big faith steps. As a

CHASE THE ROAR

church planting couple, they have navigated challenges unique to this type of ministry, all through the power of the One to whom they have devoted their lives. Ariel is currently serving as a church planter at Bedrock Church in Bozeman, Montana, where her husband Michael is the Pastor of Vision and Leadership. They have chosen to follow the call of God on their lives despite the great distance from family and loved ones and all that they have known throughout their lives. Although this is simply one example of many faith steps you'll read about in this book, it speaks volumes to the priority she places on modeling a life of faith, despite the cost.

This book is both her story and their story as a couple. It is the story of their faith walk displayed in a way that is easy for the reader to understand and emulate. She offers practical advice for ways to put her wisdom into practice. This book is for any man or woman of God seeking to grow more in your faith and, in turn, inspire your area of influence and the future generation to do the same. It will show you how to make these big faith decisions in a simple way and how to bring those you love on the journey, too.

Johnny M. Hunt

Senior Pastor, First Baptist Church, Woodstock, Georgia

INTRODUCTION

For the World Changers

"Faith is taking the first step even when you can't see the whole staircase."
—Martin Luther King, Jr.

ON THE FIRST DAY OF my freshman year at Liberty University, I was already convinced of my sole purpose for pursuing higher education. My ingenuous mind was set on becoming well-known and wealthy enough to live a comfortable life. From the time I was thirteen years old, I constructed plans to attend Liberty University (and achieve wild success there) and then go on to be a nationally-revered news anchor. I've always been driven, and my parents encouraged me in every endeavor. So I never felt that a dream *couldn't* be achieved with enough grit, hard work, and determination. Since these traits were instilled in me from my childhood, I was confident in my ability to employ them to my advantage.

CHASE THE ROAR

The problem with finding all of my strength in my own power is that I couldn't rely on this self-centered foundation for the long haul, running endless sprints in the race of life. And you don't have to be an experienced runner to know that constant sprints will burn you out. At this point in my life, my sprinting left me lost, unused, and unavailable.

What I didn't realize was that God's ambition for me during my time at college was an education in humility, enabling me to draw close to Him, allowing me to realize that I have no lasting power in my own abilities, and preparing me, instead, for the marathon runs my future would hold. My thirteen-year-old mind never predicted that the God I had happily set on the sidelines of my life would capture my heart and become the star of the field. He would demolish my plans and rebuild in my heart the desire to pursue dreams I never thought were possible to achieve through my own determination.

Our society has created a phenomenon that enables believers to seek a lifestyle that contradicts the original intention Jesus placed on Christians before His ascension into heaven. As followers of Jesus, many of us have lost sight of the Great Commission and have instead committed ourselves to pursuing a lifestyle that our world perpetuates as the best. We strive for the "American dream," instead of God's dream for our lives. In exchange for a perceived comfortable lifestyle, we sacrifice the most important attributes that help us and future generations to be healthy and

FOR THE WORLD CHANGERS

Godly human beings. Instead of being world changers, we become world followers. Just as the disciples are noted as being "men who have turned the world upside down" in Acts 17, let us be known for being dynamic influencers within our own world as we seek to change it for the Gospel!

This book is designed to encourage and equip you to follow through as a man or woman of faith, and, through your example, to influence the next generation to do the same.

The solution to our modern epidemic is for Christians to take a stand and say *enough*. Enough of following what the world says is a good and perfect person, family, or life. Enough of what society says we need in order to be happy. Enough of what our culture says we must pursue for a job. Enough of the amount of money our friends and family say is vital. We must diligently dig for the root of what the Bible highlights as important for a family of men, women, and children of great faith.

As a church-planting wife, mother of 5 babies in 6 years, lover of financial security, classic worrier, workaholic, and fan of the simple life, I have had my fair share of challenges while following this life of faith to which I have been called. I struggled with my decision to pursue ministry as a young single woman in college, and then during my early years of marriage when we never had enough money to cover the bills. We only earned $10,000 during our entire first year of marriage because we were both still in school. During the miscarriage of our first baby, I learned how to cling to the Father when my trust was shaken. And through a string of cross-country moves, including stepping out in faith to plant a church, I have learned that faith may not always make me happy, but it always makes me hopeful. People will let you down, but God?

He never fails.

Friends, we are at a crossroads. We must choose who to follow: the shallow standards set by the world or a life of faithfulness dedicated to serving the only One worthy of such devotion. This book will give you the tools and guidance to activate this plunge into a life of faith-guided freedom over the crippling and unattainable worldly standards you may be pursuing.

Whether you're a young college student, a single mom, a new father who is seeking to guide his family, a mom who is navigating the teenage years, an older man like Moses who began his ministry at 80 years old, or anything in between, this book is a guide to help you to take your faith to the next level.

As a lifelong student of faith, I'm still continuing to discover, plant, and nurture God's calling on my life. In this book, I've included time-tested steps of faith I've taken in my single life, married life, and family life. You'll learn why I do what I do and why faith is so vital to the core of who we are as a family. You'll see what this faith actually looks like in our home on a daily and weekly basis. You'll get a sense of what living a life of faith can ask of you, how to make big faith decisions, how to be a lion for Jesus in a world of wolves, how to handle financial faith, and why facing your fears is paramount.

This book is for people who fear taking the step to live free of the world's standards and abide in the true life God has for them. It is meant to be an encouragement to you, to help open your eyes to the freedom that this life in the Lord offers rather than the fear you may feel.

Throughout this book, you'll learn how to:

- ❏ Choose eternity goals over the here and now
- ❏ Discern what the call of God is in your life and your family's life
- ❏ Identify crowd followers, acceptors, and chasers
- ❏ Make big faith decisions more simple
- ❏ Take practical daily steps in your faith walk
- ❏ Include your kids in the faith journey
- ❏ Invest your money in what matters
- ❏ Minister effectively
- ❏ Cause a ripple effect

I promise that, if you follow the steps and information presented in this book, you will live a life of faith-filled freedom. God will quench the spirit of fear within you, and, at the end of your life, you will hear, "Well done, my good and faithful servant" (Matthew 25:21).

And, in doing so, you will empower the next generation to do the same.

Don't miss out on the freedom that comes from chasing a life of faith. Be the man or woman of God that people can't stop watching. Be the one people observe and join, not the one passively observing others.

If you wait to chase a life of faith and reject the guidelines found in Scripture and outlined in this book, you may miss the opportunities set before you now, and you may miss the invitation to change the course of every single person in your life.

People who experience true life change as a result of this book are the people who immediately use the tools and stories presented to ignite shifts in their lives in very concrete and specific ways. I want you to experience the freedom of living a life of authentic faith that touches your entire family. Together, let's cause the ripple that will direct generations to come!

PART ONE

Exchanging Dreams

"We must exchange whispers with God before shouts with the world."
—Lysa TerKeurst

CHAPTER ONE

Anchor in a Raging Sea

> *"Faith gives you an anchor in a raging sea, calm in the midst of chaos, vision to know right from wrong, and the courage to express it."*
>
> —*Author Unknown*

AS A TEENAGER, THIS WAS my favorite quote. Oh, how much truth is contained in a single sentence. Such beautiful, incredible truth.

I used to recite it over and over again during battles with low self-esteem, mild depression, discouragement, fear, trials, heartache, and the deep pain of moving far away from close friends. Through copious tears, I clung to it in the darkness of night. I spoke it aloud before high-pressure speaking performances that nearly strangled me, breathed it in like oxygen when weathering broken relationships, and shouted it into existence when I was uncertain of its reality in my life.

But as much as this quote meant to me as a high school student, I never imagined how it would perfectly describe my journey through adulthood.

Mobile Home

Born as the oldest child of new believers, I witnessed the very life-changing journey my parents traveled with God during my early childhood. They were married just over two years before I was born and, during that time, their lives were miraculously changed by the Gospel. Shortly after their salvation experience, they were invited to be part of what they believed to be a church plant. I was the very first baby dedicated within this brand new church. Sadly, my parents later discovered the church was born from a church split. Looking back, it's interesting to see that I began my very first church planting experience at just one week old.

When I was one year old, we made the trek across the pond to Germany for my dad's job as an electronic engineer working for the government. One year later, we returned to the U.S. where my brother was born. Shortly following his birth, we moved back to Germany, this time staying two years. Because we did not live on any type of military base, we were not constantly surrounded by Americans that would make living in a foreign country easier. From an early age, I was forced to learn how to adapt to new environments and to people who had very different beliefs. We were forced to seek out the Christians in our city and to reach out to those in our community who needed Jesus as well. This was done without the same support system we experienced in my birth state of Florida.

We relocated to Florida when I was a few weeks away from entering kindergarten. At this point, we had already made four major moves and a few other location moves within the same city during my short life. Following our return to the States, I was blessed with two little sisters born just two years apart. As an older sister to three younger siblings, I easily fell into the role of "second mom." By giving me more responsibility within our home and family, my parents instilled a confidence in me. I believed I could accomplish anything.

When I was nine, my dad was offered a position with a company in Quincy, Illinois, a tiny town on the border of Missouri and situated along the Mississippi River. We only lived in this community for fifteen months, but we lived so much *life* there. We lived on a street with twenty-three other children, all ten years old and under. We were always at a neighbor's house or playing a game of kickball together in our yard. We met several families in the community through our many activities. These friendships further solidified our family's decisions and pushed my parents to think about other ideas in a different way. Some of these ideas included what types of music we would and wouldn't listen to, which activities we would or wouldn't participate in, and which movies we would and wouldn't watch. But they also included much bigger areas of faith, like what we thought about education, how this would affect each of us growing up, and how our family functioned in relation to the world around us.

==We often won't understand what God has planned until after **we move in His will.**==

Throughout my entire childhood, I watched my parents trust in God throughout each of these decisions. Under their direction, I made these faith decisions alongside them. Their example would guide me into adulthood. When I was ten years old, we made the move from our small town in Illinois to Virginia for a job that offered my dad much less income. But my parents believed the Lord was calling them to *go*. Within a year, the company my dad previously worked for went under. Had we stayed, we would have lost everything. In that moment, I learned that ==we often won't understand what God has planned until after we move in His will.==

Rubber Meets the Road

In the fall of 2005, at eighteen years old, I embarked upon a faith journey that would carry my future family to places I never imagined. I was pursuing a degree in Broadcast Journalism, with a career goal of being a television news anchor. It was what I, and my parents, had planned for years. During that first semester, however, I quickly realized that the Lord was working in my heart. Ultimately, He would ask that I give my entire life, goals, and dreams over to Him.

One day, during that semester of constant questioning, I was sitting in a course about youth ministry. At the time, youth ministry was simply my minor and what I hoped to do on the side as I pursued my ultimate goal of being on TV. My professor, Dr. Brown, spoke about where the Lord was leading us in this specific ministry. I struggled to remember any word Dr. Brown said because all I heard was God saying, "I want something better and more amazing for you than what you are now doing. I want you to be in ministry as your *job* and not just as your side gig. I want your whole life, not just this small part."

Weeks went by as I fought with and struggled through this decision. I hid this major development from everyone I knew for fear of what they would think about me making such a dramatic change in my life. It was my little secret. I didn't know how to effectively deal with it on my own and needed the understanding ear of someone, *anyone*, in my life. But fear held me back from asking for it.

CHASE THE ROAR

A few weeks later, I walked into that same class and spoke with the professor about how I was feeling and the weight this decision carried. He, of course, encouraged me to follow God's promptings and move in the direction He led. It was then that I made the decision to change my major, and my life shifted in service to the Creator.

After this conversation, I knew it was time to let my parents know.

I was nervous. Surprisingly, they were supportive. They worried about how the decision would direct my future, but they trusted that I was truly following the Lord's leading. Trust from my loved ones made a big difference in my own soul. This was my first real, adult experience of taking big faith steps without the security of my parents to fall back on should things fall apart.

At the time of this decision, I was single, a sophomore, and I had no idea how this shift in my major would pan out. I had dreams of mentoring teen girls, serving in youth ministry, starting a conference for teen girls, or doing a multitude of other activities within ministry.

I had zero desire to actually marry a pastor, let alone a church planter.

CHAPTER TWO

The Bare Necessities

> *"I hope that when people look at my marriage, they don't think, "She has a great marriage because she chose the right guy," or, "He has a great marriage because he chose the right woman." I hope they realize, "They have a great marriage because they both chose God."*
> —Sheila Wray Gregoire

JUST TWO SHORT YEARS AFTER God redirected my career path, I stood at the altar, beaming at my 21-year-old college sweetheart. I basked in complete joy and was entirely unaware of what the Lord would ask of us in the following days.

As we were pronounced husband and wife, I took my first step of faith as wife to a man who had even more deep, trusting, gut-wrenching faith in the God he had called Savior for fifteen years.

At the time, the idea of living anywhere other than the southeastern United States was foreign. The call from God to plant a church was just beginning to take root in my heart and my husband's heart separately. In my mind, it was a more romantic idea, rather than the "live by faith no matter what" way it was capturing the heart of my new husband.

In the early years of our marriage, we were so very poor. We were both finishing our college degrees while working as much as possible. We earned a total of $10,000 during our first year of marriage. People often talk about living on love, but we were 100% living on faith alone. Even during this financially challenging time, we remained faithful in our tithe back to God. There were days we would have a bill due and have less than $20 in our bank account. I would check the mailbox only to discover an anonymous check for the exact amount we needed to pay that specific bill. God is faithful.

GOD IS Faithful

Shortly after we were married, my husband, Michael, was offered an opportunity to be a youth pastor at a church just thirty minutes down the road from our home. We were thrilled by the chance to serve in ministry together as we had been doing the past few years. But this time, it was an actual job! After serving for a few months and going on a trip with the youth group,

Michael met with the elders of the church. They explained that he was too strong of a leader for what they desired for their ministry.

We were heartbroken. We were searching for homes in the area and planning an entire life there. What was God doing with this mess?

He Opens a Window

Just a few months later, while working at Liberty University in the Visitors' Center, I learned that Dr. Johnny Hunt was scheduled to speak at the university and needed a guide for his day on campus. While that job is usually delegated to one of the student tour guides, I begged my boss to allow me to serve as his guide. You see, about a year before this, I discovered that Pastor Johnny ran a mentoring program. Every year, he took on two "mentees" to train under him, travel with him, and learn from him for the entire year. It was an opportunity that was unimaginable for someone like Michael, who felt very insignificant compared to all the pastors in the world who had vast potential. We both considered how impossible it felt that he would be chosen for this incredible opportunity, but I just *had* to meet this man. I chose to have faith that God would lead this meeting.

During Pastor Johnny's visit to Liberty, I joined him and the many college students who were from his church, First Baptist

Woodstock, and was placed directly beside him. I now recognize that this was divinely purposed by an incredible God who cares about big dreams for even little-known people like us. After this meeting, he invited us to come to his home in Georgia to interview for the mentorship program.

What?! Although we never expected Michael to receive the invitation to actually be a part of the mentorship program, considering thousands from around the country apply for it every year, the mere opportunity to spend the weekend with this incredible man of God was more than we could have imagined.

So we went. And in January of 2009, we were informed that Michael was given the opportunity to serve as a mentee under a man who would become one of the greatest mentors in his life. This was a once in a lifetime opportunity, and we realized that God was working all things out for our good according to His purpose. Of course he was. We just hadn't been able to see it from this side of heaven.

Blessings, Brokenness, and Babies

The following December, at just twenty-three and twenty-two years old, we moved to Georgia to begin what would become both one of the greatest and hardest years of our married life. Just a few months before this move, we initiated conversations about having children in the near future. This was a deep desire in each of our hearts, and we were beginning to prepare for the possibility of a pregnancy. We just thought we would have more time before our tiny dream became a reality.

In the middle of our move, Atlanta experienced a rare and dangerous snowstorm that lasted for days. The harsh weather weakened my immune system. I visited the doctor, only to find out I had developed a severe case of pneumonia. Just a few weeks later, when I went in for further testing for the pneumonia, we were surprised to find out we were expecting our first baby!

We were thrilled and terrified at the same time: thrilled that we were starting this part of our lives and terrified by how severe my pneumonia was, and by our recent move away from family to a new city.

Tragically, at our first prenatal appointment, we found out we lost that sweet baby. This sent us on a journey of unknown medical terminology, endless doctors' appointments, an MRI, discussions about adoption, one scary surgery, and more in our pursuit of answers about my miscarriage and hope for future, healthy pregnancies.

God Was Taking Care of Me, **EVEN THROUGH THE PAIN.**

Through the fog of pain and sadness, several close friends reached out to me. They shared their own stories, further confirming that, despite how I felt, God was taking care of me, even through the pain.

I underwent an HSG procedure, which involves dye being released into the body to identify any structural issues in specific areas of the body. Following that, I had an MRI, and then a 3D ultrasound. These tests confirmed that I needed surgery. I had a 90% chance of miscarrying every time I got pregnant if things remained as they were. So, just a month after digesting this difficult diagnosis, I received a surgery that was in its genesis. The doctor who performed the surgery was one of the few in the country who was trained to do so, and she just happened to be working in the city we would call our home for only a year. One month after this surgery, I became pregnant with our oldest child on earth. We were elated by such wonderful news, and once again, I was blissfully unaware of another big change on the horizon.

CHAPTER THREE

A Giant Leap

"One small step for man, one giant leap for mankind."
—*Neil Armstrong*

MOVES ARE HARD. MOVES WILL always be hard. The hardest part of moving for me is the fear of the unknown. Leaving good friends behind to pursue new friendships, giving up a financial position that is secure for one that isn't, giving up one goal for the pursuit of another. All hard and scary things. Our move from Georgia to Raleigh, North Carolina was brutal. We were taking a step of faith to help plant a church with another family we met in Georgia, only with minimal income, a new baby on the way, and just a few friends in a city we had only visited once.

Raleigh was a hard and complicated task, but one to which God called us, even though it wasn't easy. Because Michael made a very small salary of $500 a month from his ministry position, he took on a few odd jobs, all while starting his own landscaping business. The landscaping business did well, but at one point, he was working five different jobs while I worked as an online counseling professor. Even with all our efforts, we were barely able to make ends meet. Meanwhile, we were blessed with several sweet little ones very close in age. Our first two boys were born within fourteen months of one another, creating even more chaos and love in the midst of ministry and hard work. We were happy, but we were overwhelmed.

Boze... What?

After we lived, worked, served, and dreamed in Raleigh for over two years, God began to press on our hearts an intense call to move on from there. And He was already orchestrating His plan for where we would go next. Unaware of the specific vision He had for us, we began to seek out our next steps through prayer, conversations with mentors, and continuous conversations with each other.

Three years prior, while we were still living in Georgia, God spoke to our hearts about a city called Bozeman. We first heard about Bozeman through the church we were serving at in Georgia, when they received a call about the need for a pastor in this city. That was our first prompting. But then He spoke to our hearts through our individual prayer time, through relevant

Scripture that would nearly jump off of the page, and through the simple, constant communication with Him throughout our days. He confirmed it more and more through the words of great mentors in our lives. We even spoke to one mentor who had no idea we'd even heard of Bozeman. He asked Michael, "Have you ever thought about planting a church in Bozeman, Montana?"

Wow God, what a way to be very obvious.

Shortly after we made the big faith decision to follow God's lead and pursue planting a church in Bozeman, we were surprised with the news of our newest little blessing. We would have three children, two years old and under, just three months after we made the move to Montana. Fear is the biggest feeling I can recall during this time. But it wasn't the fear of the unknown as I'd previously felt, nor the fear of moving to Montana, though that did tend to creep in some days. It wasn't even the fear of having a new baby shortly after the move. I feared what others would think about us.

I Feared **WHAT OTHERS WOULD THINK ABOUT US.**

Isn't that the sad truth for so many of us? Don't we fear others' opinions even more than we fear what's actually happening in our lives? This is precisely the fear I felt: the fear of people. The type of fear Elijah felt after he defeated the

Prophets of Baal and emerged victorious for God, only to fall victim to the fear of Jezebel, just a simple woman harboring some intense hatred. In 1 Kings 19, when God asked Elijah why he was hiding in a cave, Elijah replied, "Lord God All-Powerful, I have always served you as well as I could. But the people…" (EXB).

But the people.

It's always the people that will hold us back from accomplishing the great plans God has for us.

After our first step of obedience in pursuing Montana as both our home and place of ministry, we began building financial and prayer partners for this endeavor and for Michael's "salary." This was a trying step of faith, as we had to reach out to friends, family, and churches who were a part of our lives for some time. For the first time, we publicly shared the vision for Montana and Bozeman that God imprinted on our hearts. This was hard. Not only were we asking for very specific temporal support, but we were putting all of our eggs in one basket. We asked everyone we respected and loved to support us on this journey, whether the final task was considered successful or not.

Six months after making the big faith decision to move to Montana, we hit the ground running. We moved right into a 2-bedroom 640 square foot apartment that only had running water in the bath tub at first and, for a few months, only 9 minutes of warm water. Being in my third trimester, this was not thrilling for me.

Plant Seeds

People often ask us how to plant a church. The key is to start very simply by inviting anyone you meet while out and about. So we dug right in and joined a gym, a small group, and a moms' club. We went to parks and the library. We were in the spring season of life. At that time, we only had two children to tote around as we met people, made friends, gathered a team, and joined the activities of our community. It was, in essence, the calm before the storm. We moved in late October and welcomed our third little one in January. After that, we quickly launched our first small group in March, just six weeks after our son was born.

By that summer, we began preview services. A few months after that, we had a soft launch, followed by the full launch the following Easter. As one dear friend told me, "There are people who are dessert plates and there are people who are platters and everything in between. You and I are platters, and we can't expect that everyone can handle all that we can." And boy, did I need this vote of *Solidarity* SOOTHED MY FEELINGS OF OVERWHELM AND INADEQUACY.

confidence during a time of so much busyness. Solidarity soothed my feelings of overwhelm and inadequacy.

Well into our church plant, another faith step we still take is to trust that God is in control of every single part of the plan He has for us. This has been challenged through betrayal by people we've loved dearly, in which we were left wondering where God was in the midst of it all. But He loves each of us far greater than we can imagine and He has a purpose, even when the enemy fights so hard.

Even when weary, we have to fight the good fight of faith for the Lord. The story of Elijah in 1 Kings 19 follows the great miracle the Lord performed through him when he defeated the prophets of Baal. Elijah was feeling fear, failure, a desire to die, and that this journey was too great, despite the recent victory he enjoyed. *Jesus Calling* perfectly sums up the hope we need in the midst of a difficult faith journey like the one Elijah journeyed: "You recall that not only am I with you; I am holding you by your right hand. I guide you with My counsel, and afterward I will take you into Glory. This is exactly the perspective you need; the reassurance of my Presence and the glorious hope of heaven." [1]

CHAPTER FOUR

Homesick

> *"I would have lost heart, unless I had believed that I would see the goodness of the Lord in the land of the living."*
> —Psalm 27:13 (NKJV)

TEARS SOAKED MY FACE WHILE rain soaked my body. I stood at the outdoor MercyMe concert in Philadelphia, Pennsylvania singing the song *Homesick* with thousands of others. *"If home's where my heart is then I'm out of place. Lord, won't you give me strength to make it through somehow. I've never been more homesick than now."*

These words gave my eighteen-year-old heart the freedom to cry. I felt so out of place in my current world among friends who didn't understand my Christian values. So I cried. I felt so inadequate, incapable, and utterly lost about where my life would lead. So I cried. I made poor choices in my dating relationships over the past year. So I cried.

CHASE THE ROAR

Years later, as an adult, this song would still hold emotional meaning for me when we moved our little family across the country, to a world I'd never known.

Shortly before we made the move to Montana, I wrote this in my journal:

> *"The array of emotions I have felt lately have been overwhelming for this already burdened heart...*
>
> *The questions I've asked God, the questions I've asked myself, the questions I've asked Michael...*
>
> *For a couple that is very family oriented, this is hard.*
>
> *I very distinctly remember sitting in a communications class in college and, for the first time, truly realizing what cognitive dissonance (the state of having inconsistent thoughts, beliefs, or attitudes) is and how it relates to my life; but really, this still couldn't have prepared me for the immense amount of cognitive dissonance I've experienced in the past few months and, even more so, in the past few days.*
>
> *As I was driving down the road today, as my two sick and very tired boys fell asleep, I let my mind go there.*
>
> *Honestly, I've been holding it back for quite some time.*
>
> *I let my mind go to the fact that we have permanently given our lives to the cause of Christ. This means so many things for so many people. I've questioned why, for us, that means moving over 2,000 miles away from our closest family and beloved friends. Why this means that we're called*

to Montana permanently, unless God calls us elsewhere. We're not committing for two years or five, but for life, unless God has other plans. Wrapping my mind around the thought that my sweet babies won't grow up with grandparents close by has been a hard one, but then the cognitive dissonance sets in...

And God ever so gently reminds me that He hasn't even called us to the ends of the earth or to sacrifice our very breath for Him at this time. We get to stay in America and we still have access to family via airplane, Internet, Facetime, and even simple phone calls.

So yes, while our children may miss the opportunity to go on extended family vacations, go camping with grandparents, spend time with cousins on a regular basis, or grow up in the South…

In the grand scheme of things, our sacrifice is incredibly small compared to the martyrs who have given their very lives, as well as the missionaries who have committed their lives to some very difficult groups in nations where they are hated.

The Lord has even blessed us with special little people we get to take on this new adventure with us. How lonely it would be to be alone on this journey for the Lord.

But through all of this, the cognitive dissonance rings out even more.

I'm excited, we're excited, we can't wait! We have so many hopes and dreams for our ministry in Montana, for the people there. And we already love the place, and more importantly, the people the Lord has for us to serve there.

Please be praying with us...

For our emotions.

For my worries (Admittedly, I am a struggling worry wart in the area of finances and the Lord has convicted me about this many times).

And most importantly, for our ministry.

The sacrifice, however big or small, is so worth it!

This life is not about us, and how we can be served, and how we want to live.

It is about winning people to the Lord.

So even though I may leave behind some of what society tells me should be a good life, and even though my babies may not have the extended family around I wish they could, it's not about me. And heaven will be so much sweeter because the Lord has chosen this insignificant family to sacrifice very little for the cause of Christ. Oh, heaven will be a beautiful place where we can rest and love on all who love Him."

> **This Life Is Not About Us...**
> IT IS ABOUT WINNING PEOPLE TO THE LORD.

An Eternal Perspective

Often, a faith call on our lives looks a lot different than we expect. It doesn't seem as glamorous or as easy or as beautiful as we might have imagined. While you may not be called to make a massive move to follow the specific purpose God has for your life, God may call you to people or places that are even harder for you. God may call you to stay where you are, but to follow His lead in a very different way than before. Often, doing that is much, much harder.

The most important purpose for your life is to make a difference for eternity. It is not about how well you or your family can do in this world, but how many souls you will take with you to heaven. The goal of eternity *must* be the supreme goal. Are you truly living with the end in mind? What does it even look like to live with the end in mind?

It means choosing to put others' needs above your own. It means accepting your assignment, whether it be a different city, a different job, or a different life than *you* had planned. It means choosing to invest in people instead of things. This includes all people: lost people (those who do not have a relationship with the Savior), new believers, mature believers, anyone the Lord specifically places in your life. This isn't an easy task. People and their emotions, baggage, needs, and previous wounds can even cause harm to you.

In recent history, we've witnessed a lot of hurt inflicted and damage done throughout our world. This includes many attacks on Christians, claiming we're not showing love to the marginalized. But how can we, as Christians, be what we preach and show the love of the Savior? The biggest stumbling block is selfishness. Selfishness blocks our ability to truly love and to show others that God *is* love. Selfishness destroys our ability to live out our purpose and reach people from all walks of life. It destroys our ability to lead people toward a deeper understanding of and relationship with Christ.

We can talk about how we should love and how we care and how we'd never participate in the atrocities that we're witnessing, but the best way we can show love to those who haven't been touched by the love of Jesus is by not being selfish ourselves. Show me what you do on a weekly basis and who you spend time with and I'll show you what you value. If you value yourself above all else, your week will include: your favorite hobbies or activities, your work and advancing within your job, your goals that are focused only on yourself or your family, and there will be an absence of ministry and service in the church.

Sometimes We See the Fruit

I often get homesick. That devil fights hard when we're pursuing our faith call. The only way I combat this homesickness is by witnessing lasting change in the lives of the people we're serving. I also renew my desire to see this profound change regularly through prayer and our ministry efforts. This keeps us going with our purpose.

Before we hit the ground in Montana, while we were still in the partnership building stage, one of my very best friends called me. I had been praying for her to receive Jesus for three years. And on this day, she called to tell me she was ready to ask Him to be her Savior. This was one of the very best days of my life. This was the moment for which I prayed for three years! Now, she is one of my greatest sources of comfort as we venture through the challenging days of church planting.

Oh, that God would overflow our hearts and give us so much more faith in His plan! That we would grow in love in ways you don't think possible. However minuscule and ineffective the purpose may feel when it is given to us, we can rest in the certainty that God is all-knowing and all-powerful. He has already written the pages of our life story. We just have to live it.

HE HAS ALREADY WRITTEN THE PAGES OF OUR LIFE STORY. We Just Have to Live It.

But how do we do this? How do we make life decisions out of faith? How do we entrust our whole selves to Jesus? Let's dive in to some of the ways you can make your own faith journey a reality in your life. We'll start at the beginning, with the call of God on your life, and how to discover and follow individual faith steps you'll need to take to determine the path for your life.

PART TWO

The Chase

> "...but those who hope in the Lord will renew their strength. They will soar on wings like eagles; they will run and not grow weary, they will walk and not be faint."
>
> —*Isaiah 40:31*

CHAPTER FIVE

Plankton and the Ocean Current

> *A missionary is someone who leaves their family for a short time so that others may be with their families for eternity.*
> —*Author Unknown*

IN APRIL 2013, I GAZED out the window of the airplane as we began our ascent out of Bozeman one final time before we return as permanent missionaries just a few months later. Barely able to catch my breath through the tears, I was most heartbroken over my children growing up far away from grandparents, family, and loved ones who deeply care for them.

Shortly following this moment of sadness and pity, a close friend shared a quote with me: "A missionary is someone who leaves their family for a short time so that others may be with their families for eternity" (Author Unknown).

Oh, that my heart would know the searing pain of death without eternity with the Father! Only then would I refuse to waste such precious moments feeding my own desires and working to catapult myself to a place that, in my mind, is better for me and in turn rejects God's plan for my life.

Passion and Plankton

I once heard a story told by Sadie Robertson of the Duck Dynasty family. It made my heart ache. I was reminded that I must be faithful even in the worst of situations. While our missionary journey certainly wasn't the worst of situations, I was encouraged when Sadie shared the definition of plankton she discovered on Wikipedia: "a small microorganism unable to swim against the current of the ocean that provides food for big fish and whales to eat."

"Is there anything worse than being plankton?" she thought. Then, she had a revelation:

> "But God was like, what if you were plankton? Are they really the lowest of the low? Could you find passion and

PLANKTON AND THE OCEAN CURRENT

could you find purpose in something that seems so low, but something that I gave life to?"[2]

She went on to explain that plankton float and are unable to swim against the current. In the Greek language, the word *plankton* actually means "to wander" or "to be a wanderer." Plankton find their genesis at the very bottom of the ocean, in the darkest part, where all of the life forms surrounding them are trying to eat them. Slowly, they make their way to the top of the ocean in order to receive the light needed for photosynthesis. But then, they don't stay in the light where it is safe. They go back down to the bottom, they return to everything that wants to eat them, and they provide 90% of the ocean's photosynthesis and 50% of the oxygen that we breathe. Sadie determined that this is what passion does. Passion gives you the fuel to press past your fear in order to fulfill the purpose that God has for you.

Passion Gives You the Fuel to Press Past Your Fear IN ORDER TO FULFILL THE PURPOSE THAT GOD HAS FOR YOU.

This is exactly where we all need to be as followers of Christ; but even more so, as people of faith with a passion to see the lost come to faith, no matter the cost.

Answering the Call

The core premise of why my family does what we do is because eternity is far more important than messing around with the unimportant things that pale in comparison. It is the overarching goal, the highest priority, and the God-given plan for all of our lives as believers. The call of God on our life is *the* reason we are placed on this earth.

We want our children to grow up knowing that faith, church family, and sharing Jesus are the most important aspects of their lives. We want them to understand that life is short and eternity is vital for their sake and the sake of others. That, if we allow them to invest all their time and energy in activities and sports while neglecting church, fellowship with believers, and sharing Jesus with the lost, then we have not prepared them for a future of following Jesus.

Dear ones, when you're feeling exactly like plankton, floating with the current of the ocean, being chased by the big fish and whales, go back to your purpose. At the end of your life, will you hear, "Well done, good and faithful servant!"? Will we hear this because we have financially spoiled our families and given our time and effort to meaningless activities, or because we have been faithful in everything the Lord has asked of us?

People often ask us, what *exactly* is a call of God, and how do we know what it is?

PLANKTON AND THE OCEAN CURRENT

There is a general call of God on all believers' lives. This would be similar to the process of the plankton. When they reach the light, they take it back down to the depths, where they share photosynthesis with the rest of the creatures in the sea. Once we have received salvation, we are immediately called to go back to those who are lost and share the light with them. The main call of God on our lives is the Great Commission: to make disciples of all nations, baptizing them and teaching them how to obey His commands (Matthew 28:19-20).

Luke 4:18-19 declares, "The Spirit of the Lord is on me, because he has anointed me to bring good news to the poor. He has sent me to proclaim freedom for the prisoners and recovery of sight for the blind, to set the oppressed free, to proclaim the year of the Lord's favor."

Jesus calls us to reconciliation and liberation. So yes, we have some ideas about what we should be doing as Christians. But how does this look, specifically in relation to the call of God on our personal lives?

There are 3 basic steps to take in the process of determination:

1. Discover the call on your personal life.
2. Follow that call faithfully.
3. Continue to follow the call.

These 3 steps are so simple, but are so often forgotten in the midst of our day-to-day lives and amidst challenges that accompany the call. Even during the writing of this book, I have employed this exact process. For years, God called me to write a book. I even started and stopped the book writing process several times over those years. But I was completely unaware that this specific call on my personal life reached beyond my married life, our life in ministry together, and my calling as a mom.

This is where the first step in this process comes into play. We have to actually discover the call on our personal life before we can pursue it. This involves actively listening when God is speaking. For years, I ignored the tender and quiet spirit of God urging me toward writing. Even just a few weeks before I began writing, I blocked it from my mind, believing it was an impossible feat. Many mornings I woke after experiencing dreams about the specific purpose God had for this book, the topics that would be included, and the Scripture He was pressing on my heart. I turned to the Bible, prayer, and my husband as I worked out the details of exactly what was being asked of me. I felt vulnerable when I shared this call on my life with a few close friends and mentors, but I determined that this was exactly where I was being led. So, in fear, I pushed ahead.

Once you've determined your call, the second step is following that call faithfully. To me, faithfully, means dedicating all that God has given me to that task. This means giving up little things that I may enjoy or inconveniencing myself to be sure I continue following through. In order to chase the call to write a book, it meant giving up sleep, changing my schedule, sacrificing down time for a few months, and cultivating determination and grit. I faithfully followed this call from God by giving up the things I consider enjoyable and relaxing in order to serve this greater purpose. When it comes to continuing to follow this specific call to write what God asks me to share, I have to continuously go back to prayer and conversations when I feel the desperate need to give up.

I also followed this process of determination when I began the children's ministry at our church plant. I can tell you that I did not, for one second, feel inclined to begin this ministry by my own free will. My heart fought it hard. I realized this was the call of God on my life, even if for a short season, because there was no one else who was able to fill this need we had in our church. And God was asking *me* to do it. But isn't that how it often is? Sometimes, it isn't a beautifully orchestrated plan with bells ringing and God's voice booming telling you to *do it*. Often, it is just you, as a humbled servant, seeing the need, asking God for confirmation, and then going and doing what you are supposed to do. That's exactly how uncovering this call looked for me. Now, following the call faithfully as well as continuing to follow the call have nearly wrecked me emotionally and spiritually several times over the past few years. At first, following the call faithfully meant that I was the one in charge of scheduling, curriculum prepping, printing, finding volunteers, and orchestrating every little component of every single Sunday morning children's worship service. I continued to follow this call by training and teaching others who could eventually carry this load with me. This did not mean I would be finished serving or leading the children's ministry, but it meant that I was bringing others along with me to learn, grow, and serve in this way.

Determining the call may seem like the most challenging aspect at the time. But in reality, continuing to follow the call when the waters get murky and you feel your life is in disarray is truly the hardest part. It's all about perspective. Do you see each person around you the way the Father sees them and loves them unconditionally? It's about perspective when it comes to choice-making. Is every choice made through the lens that Jesus has granted us as believers? The ultimate motive behind everything, even on our hardest, scariest, most devastating days, is to invest in eternity.

IT'S ALL ABOUT *Perspective*

Later, in the Big Faith, Bigger God chapter, I'll touch on the Faith Challenge I include below. You can use this process every time you take a new faith step within your journey. This faith step should always coincide with the call of God on your life. For now, I'll mention it here for your reference:

The Faith Challenge

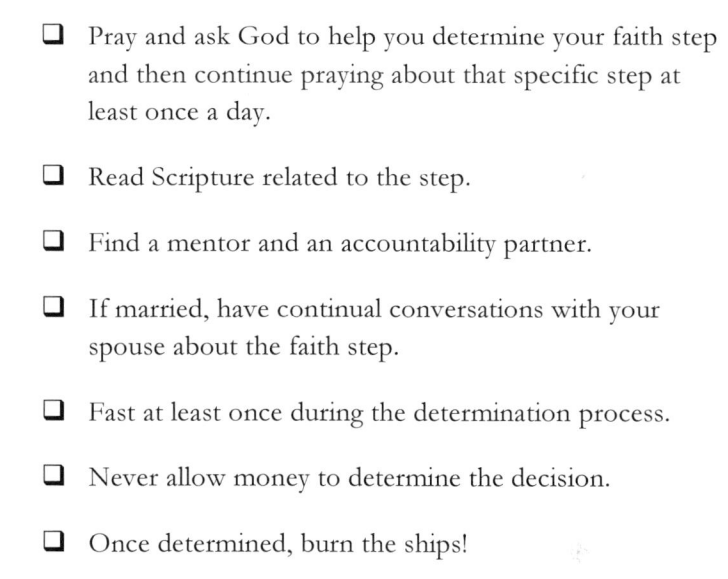

- ❏ Pray and ask God to help you determine your faith step and then continue praying about that specific step at least once a day.
- ❏ Read Scripture related to the step.
- ❏ Find a mentor and an accountability partner.
- ❏ If married, have continual conversations with your spouse about the faith step.
- ❏ Fast at least once during the determination process.
- ❏ Never allow money to determine the decision.
- ❏ Once determined, burn the ships!

Throughout Scripture, and especially in daily quiet time and prayer, Jesus shows us how to understand the call He has on our particular lives and how to follow that call. But we also know that, as followers of Christ, we must bear fruit for God to continue being used. Later in this book, you'll be encouraged to go through a spiritual gifts inventory that will enable you to better understand your specific gifts and talents. This will help you use those gifts and talents to bring glory to the Father.

CHASE THE ROAR

In one of the parables Jesus used to illustrate the things of God to common people, He shares the story of a man who gave his servants talents according to their own abilities. I'm sure you have heard this before, but quiet your heart now as you consider this truth in your own life:

> *"To one he gave five talents, to another two, to another one, to each according to his ability. Then he went away. He who had received the five talents went at once and traded with them, and he made five talents more. So also he who had the two talents made two talents more. But he who had received the one talent went and dug in the ground and hid his master's money. Now after a long time the master of those servants came and settled accounts with them. And he who had received the five talents came forward, bringing five talents more, saying, 'Master, you delivered to me five talents; here, I have made five talents more.' His master said to him, 'Well done, good and faithful servant. You have been faithful over a little; I will set you over much. Enter into the joy of your master.' And he also who had the two talents came forward, saying, 'Master, you delivered to me two talents; here, I have made two talents more.' His master said to him, 'Well done, good and faithful servant. You have been faithful over a little; I will set you over much. Enter into the joy of your master.' He also who had received the one talent came forward, saying, 'Master, I knew you to be a hard man, reaping where you did not sow, and gathering where you scattered no seed, so I was afraid, and I went and hid your talent in the ground. Here, you have what is yours.' But his master answered him, 'You*

wicked and slothful servant! You knew that I reap where I have not sown and gather where I scattered no seed? Then you ought to have invested my money with the bankers, and at my coming I should have received what was my own with interest. So take the talent from him and give it to him who has the ten talents. For to everyone who has will more be given, and he will have an abundance. But from the one who has not, even what he has will be taken away." (Matthew 25:15-29, ESV).

Chase Your Faith:

God clearly rewards faith in our lives. You may be feeling a bit like the servant who received the one talent and was afraid to use it, or even touch it, for fear that you are not good enough. You may hide it away from others so that they can't know what God has for your life. But at what risk? At what cost? At the cost of Jesus deeming you a lazy servant?

What is a talent in your life right now that you are *not* using to further the Kingdom? Ask yourself how you are specifically furthering the Kingdom at this point in your life. What are some ways you can actually begin doing this today? What are some goals you can set for yourself this week?

CHASE THE ROAR

We have just begun to unearth some of the vital steps you will take as a man or woman of faith in determining the call of God on your life, and how this will affect you as you seek to serve Him in even more specific ways. Let's continue on together as we identify some of the different types of believers and how you can use this perspective to change the trajectory of your life.

CHAPTER SIX

Chase the Roar

> *"Benaiah son of Jehoiada, a valiant fighter from Kabzeel, performed great exploits. He struck down Moab's two mightiest warriors. He also went down into a pit on a snowy day and killed a lion."*
> —2 Samuel 23:20

IT WAS 6 AM ON a Sunday morning in May 2010. I woke up to the most horrific sound. The roar of a freight train coming at me. Still believing I was in a nightmare, I jumped up, along with everyone around me. I had been staying with several college roommates and friends following a dear college friend's wedding. We began racing for the cellar that we knew was under the house. Blind, because I didn't have my contacts in and didn't take the time to grab my glasses, we lifted the cellar door only to find that it was completely flooded. By this time, the sound had passed. We knew exactly what it was. One of many tornadoes

CHASE THE ROAR

that was sure to come with the catastrophic storm that had hit. We sat there for a few minutes pondering our next move.

We knew it would be best to jump into the flooded cellar and swim until it passed if it returned, but it didn't. In silence, we contemplated our next move. Eventually, we jumped up to survey the damage outside. The tornado had barely missed us, ripping across the front yard of the home we were staying in. But the flood was rising. We knew staying in the house would prove to be potentially more damaging to us, but going out into the storm meant we'd be chasing tornadoes. We chose the option to get out of town. While it may not have been our brightest idea, staying would have meant enduring a flood. As we took off in our separate cars, a few of us in each one, we fought to get onto the highway that would get us out of town. After finally merging onto the highway, we looked back to see that there were several tornadoes touching down in different parts of the city. Praising God for our escape, we managed to get a few more minutes down the road before realizing we were driving parallel to several more tornadoes that we could see on the other side of the large field. There were only three of us in the vehicle at that time, but we

> IT'S OFTEN SAFER TO *Chase the Roar* OF DANGER THAN TO REMAIN WHERE THE WATERS ARE CALM, BUT RISING.

decided should the tornadoes shift and come in our direction, we would pull off the road and huddle in the ditch. By the grace of God, we managed to escape without any issues, but it's a story that will forever be etched into our memories. Throughout this experience, I learned that it's often safer to chase the roar of danger than to remain where the waters are calm, but rising.

Snow-Filled Pits

The book of Samuel tells the story of the Old Testament hero Benaiah, son of Jehoida, who was a famous warrior. He became known for chasing a lion into an icy, snow-filled pit where he killed it and emerged victorious.

Only one verse in 2 Samuel mentions him, but references to Benaiah and his heroic feats appear throughout the Old Testament. I love when the Bible mentions, even if briefly, people who displayed great courage. Ordinary people who God used in an extra-ordinary way. Or-dinary people who were obedient to God throughout their entire life. People like David, Abraham, Daniel, Moses, Joshua,

OUR GOD IS A GOD OF *Bravery, Courage, and Victory.*

Rahab, Paul, Nehemiah, and Deborah. Our God is a God of bravery, courage, and victory. He is a God of all the things my boys aspire to: boldness in battle, defeating mighty bears and lions, and finishing victoriously. He's not a God who sits idly by, laughing at us and allowing us to fight by our own strength. This means that, even I, during my meekest moments, can actively pursue great feats of strength with courage.

Three Types of Believers

I've discovered there are three types of believers when it comes to living out faith: followers, acceptors, and chasers. Each of us have likely fit into one of these categories at different times, and we may fluctuate between them, depending on the day.

A follower is, essentially, a crowd pleaser. This is the person whose faith is built on peer pressure. Many of us experienced this in childhood and adolescence and, still often, as adults. A follower invests in their faith when it's cool, romantic, or popular. This is often the case following retreats, large conferences, major faith gatherings, or even among smaller groups of people within the church. According to the Webster's New World College dictionary, "groupthink" is the tendency of those within a group to follow the most popular opinion within the group.[3] A follower is never the leader and doesn't actually make the decision, but takes the faith step if, and only if, groupthink is involved.

A follower does not necessarily live out their own faith, but the generalized activity of faith. I was a quintessential follower throughout my high school years. I followed my peers in big faith steps while on a spiritual high during or immediately following a retreat. These big faith steps included participating in major service projects together and decisions to give up areas of our lives that we desperately wanted to cling to. In high school, this meant not spending time with certain people or on different social media outlets, or not going to parties where alcohol was served. Together, at the retreat, we committed to several days of fasting, and we shared the Gospel in very public places. But when it came time to live out my faith among the lost around me, I quickly clung to my fear and pride. While the lost around me knew I was a Christian, it didn't actually change my life in a genuine way.

Being a follower isn't necessarily a bad thing. It can actually be a very good thing, as the disciples themselves were followers of Jesus. If you are following the right people, you can glean a great deal. It can, in fact, be very beneficial for society to have people willing to learn from and follow those who are godly leaders. At some point, however, we also have to ensure this is not leading us away from our specific call from God. We cannot make every single faith decision based on what everyone else is doing. If we do not make strides past this realm, we can be held captive to the crowd instead of making an individual faith move.

Think for a minute about some of the ways you may be a follower in your life. Are you following what the group surrounding you is doing? Are you making decisions apart from those you may be following? How is being a follower at this present moment in your life benefiting you or leading you away from your personal call?

Acceptors are believers who always play it safe on their faith journey. Similar to athletes in a sport who will step up to the plate *only* if continuously encouraged by their coach, and *only* with certainty that it will all work out, so are the acceptors when it comes to a life of faith. They view life, and their faith, as being a choice. They may accept the challenge or they may not. Acceptors pray for more faith, but question God when He actually shows them what to do. They aspire to do great things, but constantly question whether God is really asking them to take that first step. I would venture to say that this is the category many of us find ourselves when deeply aspiring to live a life of faith. It is where apathy reigns and where we believe we're true followers of God. But it really means we're relying on our own ideas, plans, and choices. It is the place where actual hope dies.

How often do you wake up in the morning and ask God to show up and show you what you're supposed to do? Do you have loved ones around you who believe God is telling you to accept a specific challenge or to give something up? Do you then completely refuse this notion? What life-altering steps of faith have you taken in the past month? In the past year? Whatever you do, please do not let fear be a hindrance to you. Don't compare yourself to stories found within this book or any others and think, "I just can't do that." Faith grows *with* you. Just take each faith step with obedience and do not let comparison hinder you from experiencing what God has just for you.

Faith Grows **WITH YOU.**

Chasers are believers who run after their faith, just like Benaiah did when he chased the lion into the snowy pit. The lion clearly had the upper hand at close to 500 pounds, with vision that is five times better than that of a human possessing 20/20 vision. In a pit of ice and snow, this man, while a warrior, was at a severe disadvantage as he faced the lion with claws and reflexes made for just this type of battle.

This is what faith chasers do. They take the first step and venture down to the pit, even if they are at a clear disadvantage. They don't have to know the end result. They don't have to see the whole picture. They're not following because someone went before them, or accepting it only if they are fully convinced it will all work out. Of course, those who chase will sometimes fail, but they always, always get back up. They fear God more than they fear failure. If only we would aspire to be a chaser of faith in every single moment of every single day! If only we would refuse to hide in fear at the roar of the lion, and instead face it head on.

Chase Your Faith:

Think about ways you may or may not be a chaser. How are you chasing after the dream God has given you? How are you purging fear and choosing to trust over everything else? How are you chasing your purpose even if there is the possibility of failure? Oh, that we would be bold in our faith for others watching us, for the sake of our families! None of us are completely there yet, but don't give up the chase! James 1:4 speaks about this. "Let perseverance finish its work so that you may be mature and complete, not lacking anything."

We will never be fully mature or complete until God calls us home, but we have to persevere. How are you persevering with every single faith step today? How can you start this now if you haven't yet?

_____

_____

_____

_____

CHASE THE ROAR

Chasers don't settle for making one big faith decision to last them for a few weeks or months or years. They are always looking for the next chase. My prayer for myself, for you, dear reader, for my children, for my church, and for my city, is that more believers would be chasers. Those who chase the lion even on the snowiest of days. I pray that we will see God for who He is, the One who knows the future, who goes before us, who is already victorious in the battle. I pray that our hearts would know the heart of the Father and His desires for our lives. Let's boldly proclaim to the world that we aren't afraid to chase the biggest, most unfathomable faith step God has required of us. Let's figure out how to do this in our daily lives.

CHAPTER SEVEN

All Your Might

> *"Whatever your hand finds to do, do it with all of your might..."*
> —*Ecclesiastes 9:10*

WALKING THE HALLS OF MY kindergarten school, following my dad during school pickup, I would regularly encounter exactly two quarters on the ground in front of me. This was the exact amount of change needed for the soda machine at school. The soda machine held my favorite grape soda with all its bubbly goodness. I couldn't figure out how I would find exactly two quarters so frequently. I thought I must be the luckiest kid ever to find such a treasure at least once a week! Years later, I learned that it was my dad who carefully dropped this precious change as he walked in front of me. Growing up as his daughter, I learned two very important lessons. I learned that, if my dad loved to give good gifts to my siblings and me, how much more does my heavenly Father love to give good and precious gifts? Additionally, I learned that a hard work ethic, along with a little fun, will get you a long way in life. You see, my dad is probably the hardest worker I know, and I have found that it is in the hard working heroes that I find the greatest inspiration for how to live my life.

Heroes in the Daily Living

Often, we sing the praises of mighty warriors in the Bible, or even those in our world today who are known for their triumphant feats for Jesus. But it is often in the very ordinary and mundane parts of life that we see the true testament of God's faithfulness. In fact, the entire book of Psalms shows David as a man who had the very same struggles and strengths that we encounter on a daily basis. And he recorded them for us to recite and proclaim over these very same battles we face day in and day out.

In fact, Thomas Chisholm wrote the song "Great is Thy Faithfulness" as a proclamation to the faithfulness of God in his very ordinary life. At the end of his life, Chisholm declared, "My income has not been large at any time due to impaired health in the earlier years which has followed me on until now. Although I must not fail to record here the unfailing faithfulness of a covenant-keeping God and that He has given me many wonderful displays of His providing care, for which I am filled with astonishing gratefulness."[4]

The biggest challenge doesn't always manifest when the faith step is being determined, but often well after you are on the path. The faith step I have mostly addressed in this book is the major one that led to ministry in Montana: real, hard, down on your knees in prayer, dirty type of ministry. Although we still have to take faith steps on at least a weekly basis, they all find their origin and purpose in our first call, our first "yes" to Montana. Below, I'll show you how we are chasing faith on a daily and weekly basis in our home and lives. After that, we'll focus on how you can determine how each part of your life falls into your faith step.

Our Daily Lives

Because our faith step involves our entire family and not just the adults, we involve the kids in these ways:

Bible Reading

This might be a "duh" statement for some, but we have found that this does not take top priority for many families. As a ministry family, we cannot lose sight of the first priority in our lives. We don't want to serve on empty. We want to be filled and equipped to go out. We intentionally read the Bible by ourselves in the morning and throughout the day, and to our kids most nights. Yes, there are nights when we get home past bedtime and everyone is barely crawling in to bed. But, for the most part, this is a routine that is vital in our family life. This not only helps our kids to understand God's purpose for their lives and His purpose for us as believers; but it also helps us, as parents, to keep a focus on our top priority in the midst of busy ministry. What are some ways you can apply this within your own family life?

> **WE DON'T WANT TO SERVE**
> *On Empty.*

ALL YOUR MIGHT

Sharing Jesus with the Lost and Inviting Others to Church

I've had several constructive conversations with my kids after leaving an outing or play date. They wonder why certain people have said the things they've said, and why I shared what I did. One day, we were at a park for about an hour and, during this time, we had a woman share with us that she didn't believe in church and a solid community of believers. I gently explained to her what it says in the Bible about church and how vital it is to living out our faith. She had a clear misunderstanding of the purpose of a church community and the goals that can be accomplished through it. My kids were trying to grasp why she was so bitter about church, and I lovingly reminded them that not everyone understands the purpose of church, and that's why it's important that we share why we love it!

Another day, visitors came to our house to share some of the things they believe about the Bible that are not even found in Scripture. My children knew this and were so confused about the purpose of their visit. They observed as I spoke to these women in a kind and firm way, explaining why we believe what we believe and where it can actually be found in the Bible. My kids now have more confidence when speaking with their own friends about these issues.

In turn, this has created a foundation to share with them what absolute truth is, why I believe it, and why it is important to explain that to others. As a result, we've witnessed our oldest children sharing this truth with kids their own age as well! I take the opportunity to have these encounters with others at the park, museum, my kids' activities, school-related events, and even in church, where I serve many children who are lost. But you may find that sharing Jesus begins within your work place, school, gym, activities, or stores that you frequent. I'll be honest, it seems terribly awkward when you take that first step and invite that first person, but with each new invitation comes a level of confidence and purposefulness that propels you on to invite the next and the next and the next. Inviting someone to church is also far less intimidating because it's just that, an invitation. You are gifting someone with something that will not only help them, but their entire family. You are not taking anything from anyone. You are sharing your love for your church family with them.

It is often much harder to invite someone I know personally rather than the stranger at the grocery store. I fear their opinion of me after the fact. But inviting a friend who knows me is far more successful! I have a friend who I knew for a year prior to her attending our church. We talked about her concerns. I was there, as a listening ear, and she knew that the invitation was always extended to visit our church. When she eventually came with her family, the growth process began and it has been incredible to witness. I am deeply grateful that God took the time to cultivate this friendship.

On the flip side, I had another experience that was very different from this one. I finally worked up the courage to invite a dear friend to our church. When I extended the invitation, I took a few minutes to explain why I believed what I believed. We entered into a deep conversation which concluded with her declaration that she would never become a Christian or attend church. She emphasized her desire to remain close friends. Of course we remained friends, and I continued to speak freely about my testimony and listen to her as well. Often, it takes several attempts and quite a bit of effort or traumatic experience to get someone to the point of acceptance. But, I'm there for the long haul if it means one more for the kingdom. And, even if it doesn't, at least I loved them until the end.

Inviting people to church can happen anywhere. Just recently, I met a kind woman in Costco with a few boys in tow and we started chatting about our families. Toward the end, I simply said, "I don't know if you are attending church anywhere, but my husband is a pastor at this church, and we'd love if you would attend. We've got a great children's ministry and a great church family." She gladly welcomed the invitation and it was as simple as that.

Thom Ranier found that "Ninety-six percent of the unchurched are at least somewhat likely to attend church if they are invited. Perhaps we need to pause on this response. Perhaps we need to restate it. More than nine out of ten of the unchurched said they would come to church if they were invited."[5]

It's all about the heart. Since personal invitations by church members is the number one reason the unchurched step foot in a church, it is up to us to do our part to facilitate this opportunity. How can you be more of a facilitator of this within your community? What changes can you make to ensure this becomes and remains a priority?

Meeting with People in our Church and Community

One of the important qualities that has been instilled in our kids through this process is the ability to recognize that life is not always about their wants and desires. This lesson is the same for myself as an adult. Would my boys prefer that all of their play dates be with friends their age? Of course they would. But they recognize that sometimes, when we get together with people, it is more about pouring into them. I often spend time with women who may not have children, or who have children in a completely different age group than mine, and I've had to talk with my boys about the purpose and goals for this. This is the same if you are a single adult working to serve with purpose. You may only desire to spend time with people who you enjoy being with, but God has called us to reach out to even those we may not be particularly fond of.

> *God Has Called Us to Reach out*
> TO EVEN THOSE WE MAY NOT BE PARTICULARLY FOND OF.

Recently, the kids in our elementary ministry at church learned about showing respect to others (the favoritism principle) as seen in James 2:1-4, 8-9:

> *"My brothers and sisters, believers in our glorious Lord Jesus Christ must not show favoritism. Suppose a man comes into your meeting wearing a gold ring and fine clothes, and a poor man in filthy old clothes also comes in. If you show special attention to the man wearing fine clothes and say, "Here's a good seat for you," but say to the poor man, "You stand there" or "Sit on the floor by my feet," have you not discriminated among yourselves and become judges with evil thoughts? If you really keep the royal law found in Scripture, "Love your neighbor as yourself," "you are doing right. But if you show favoritism, you sin and are convicted by the law as lawbreakers."*

Wow, convicted as lawbreakers? That's brutal. And often, when we read passages from the Bible like this, it is hard for us to relate them to our lives when it discusses a man wearing fine clothes and a gold ring. But really, it comes down to us giving up a bit of our comfort to spend time with those who may not be *just like us* or enjoy the things we do. If you are a man of God leading your family toward Him, consider befriending the man who isn't leading his family. If you are a woman with a very full plate, consider meeting with a mom who is struggling to make it through each day.

Who in your neighborhood, your school, your church, your job, or anywhere else in your community would you not necessarily choose to spend time with? How can you meet them where they are? How can you love on them despite their differences that may frustrate you? Be sure to write those names down now and reach out to them in love, displaying your hatred of favoritism. Show your community how the church can be a light in a dark place and a comfort for all who come, not only for those who are well-liked by certain people.

In full transparency, I admit I have often struggled in dealing with hardened hearts while continuing to share Jesus and invite those hardened hearts to be a part of our church family. But then, I have found that God shows me the places in my own heart that are hardened and how He is working to chip away at these sentiments. So I continue to invite, share, and love on those people who have shut themselves off from the Gospel, the church, people within our church family, or our immediate family.

Serving First as a Priority, Even Within Our Family

To serve first, even within our family, means that our sons are required to help us around the house and church when they'd rather be doing something else. My six year old wakes himself up each morning. He can prepare breakfast, get the youngest boys up and dressed, feed the dog, and clean his room without guidance from us. The younger ones are learning to do the same. Even though this may seem like a small thing, they are contributing to the bigger calling of our family by helping with the day-to-day tasks. I often hear from parents that raising young children makes for an overwhelming season. They think this does not leave room in their lives to serve. This is a tragedy for not only those who are missing out on being served, but for their family and children. As an adult, what are some ways you are focused on serving as first priority before your own personal desires? How can you better put your faith life on display by serving within your daily tasks?

___

If you are a parent, and especially if you stay at home with your kids, let's look at some ways you can "hack" your home systems to enable margins for service. Even with younger children, a busy career, college classes, or anything else in life that feels a bit crazy at this time, you can still make some positive changes in this area. But you will have to actually build time in your weekly or daily schedule. For my family, this means I cannot be at their beck and call every second of every day. My children understand this, and I am ultimately doing them a service by preparing them to be independent, even in some small ways at their very young ages. My children are involved with our chores and home structure so that it does not all fall to me. This enables us all to serve at church, in our community, and in our home.

ALL YOUR MIGHT

I'm going to share a little about our system, but I want you to know that I do not have it all together. I haven't learned all I need to in this area. I am always open for suggestions and opportunities to grow. My children are the ones responsible for picking up their toys, their room, their clothes, and transferring dirty clothes to the laundry room. We generally do a quick clean up twice a day, including once before or immediately following lunch and once in the evening before bed. I say generally, as there are times when we are away from home. In these instances, we may have one slightly longer clean up during the day. My oldest three are also responsible for getting themselves dressed in the morning and fastening both themselves and our youngest into their car seats before we leave. If my children did not do these seemingly small tasks each morning to help our family function, we would never make it to the places we need to be and to the people we need to be serving.

Because we recently made the decision to begin homeschooling, our schedule is changing a bit. I am now required to spend some mornings at home to teach, when I used to spend that time meeting with other moms or other women within our community. Now, I have to create margin in other places, like our evenings. Often, "hacking" your home system means that you may not be able to cook an incredible meal that takes hours to prepare every single night. Often, it means making a simple dinner of sandwiches and fruit and being OK with that, since it serves a far greater purpose to the overall goals of your family or life of ministry.

If you are someone with a busy career or if you are in college, but do not have children yet, this can apply to you. You may need to allocate certain evenings each week to different things to keep your home life and ministry running. If you work a full-time job, stay at home with children, are in school, or involved in anything else that requires a large portion of your day, consider your schedule. Could you set aside one evening to catch up on chores, one evening for a Life group, home group, or small group, one evening for preparing dinners for the week, and one evening for serving in some type of ministry together as a family or an individual? If you do have young children, all of these things could be done together, with their help. This would take up about four evenings of your week, leaving a few more evenings for outside activities you enjoy and errands. Write down some ideas.

ALL YOUR MIGHT

Think through your specific call and how you can make this the focus of your daily life, taking precedence over your job, activities, and other responsibilities. For us, our faith call as a family plays a vital role in our lives because it is a part of our daily schedule and not perceived as an additional inconvenience. Do you filter every activity you are involved with through this call? This is not to say that you cannot build some margin into your schedule for fun, for activities you enjoy, for people you love and cherish, and for time alone with your family. These are all good and necessary things. Times of rest and enjoyment should be built into your schedule as well, but let's first be great stewards of our time and cherish the things, people, and ministries that matter to God. What are three ways your faith call can be displayed on a daily basis?

Weekly Basis

On a weekly basis, we have several non-negotiable ministry activities, and we're working to ensure that our boys understand that these are things we do to serve God and people over ourselves, even on the days we "don't feel like it." This instills qualities in them that will not only help them in the ministry world, but in the secular world as well. We must learn to be "doers" of the Word, and not just hearers. And in the world of business, we often have to follow through even though we may not feel like it, simply because we've committed to it. As a family who is following a specific faith call on our lives, we do evaluate every area in our lives where time is given to ensure that we are following a specific purpose; therefore, things may change with the seasons. However, a lot of prayer and guidance from mentors leads us to the decisions we make regarding where our efforts are most needed to best build the Kingdom and show His glory.

Bible Studies and Life Group

For now, I attend a weekly women's Bible study and we host a Life Group at our home each week. Our church calls our small groups that meet in host homes "Life Groups" because the intention is to "do" life together. We share a meal together, study the Bible, hang out together, and serve together. These are two of the gatherings we've placed on our schedule with a purpose. We also invite others to spend time with us at these places and we've formed wonderful, refreshing, life-giving relationships. We see that we are needed by God in these places for this moment in time. What are some potential groups like this that you could be involved with on a weekly basis? Sharing life together within a small group is vitally important to your health as an individual, family, and as a group of believers. Start conversations with those in your church and community about the potential opportunity to do life together in this way.

Set Up/Tear Down

Because our church is a church plant, we meet in a school every Sunday. This means we are required to do set up and tear down each week. This is another space where our entire family serves on a weekly basis. And we ask that as many as possible within the church do the same. This has also been a place where I can teach our kids why we do this and how this helps others to receive the message of Jesus each week. Often, when we are doing the mundane things in life that take so much hard work, it is easy to become frustrated and lose sight of the overarching purpose, so I've had many conversations with our kids explaining how preparing a place for individuals and families to come worship allows them to more easily open their hearts to God.

If you are not a part of a church plant within your community, consider some ways that you could serve in the established church together as a family. Could you arrive early and help prepare the children's ministry material? Could you ensure that all materials for the main service are prepared? Could you volunteer with hospitality and serve coffee together? Consider some ways you could potentially be a part of the "set up" and "tear down" crews even within a church that has a large portion of these details covered by staff. Ask those in leadership how your family can serve together to enable the weekend experiences to go more smoothly. This enables both you and those in your family to recognize that it's about leading people to Jesus more than it is about our personal comfort. Write down some of these ideas now.

ALL YOUR MIGHT

Helping at the Ministry Hub

We also help with the ministry hub at our church. We recently established this "ministry hub" as a place to serve, grow, and learn apart from the Sunday morning experience. It is a place for us to do ministry during the week. It is a place for youth events, staff meetings, leadership nights, and preparation for Sunday morning to take place.

Some of the preparation that my children are a part of is the work that is done for our kids' ministry. While this may not take place every week, we attend as needed to help with printing, preparing, or helping with others. They can then see how the work done throughout the week serves our kids on Sunday mornings and the motivation behind it. This has given our kids the chance to see ministry firsthand while providing a concrete example of the time and effort that goes into sharing Jesus with the kids at our church each week. This helps all of us further value that work. What opportunities are available at your church? Are there ministries throughout the week you could assist with, even in preparation for them, if not for the actual events? How can you involve your kids in the children's ministry within your church that directly benefits them and their friends?

___

Church Attendance as Priority Over Activities

We've had to explain to our children why they cannot be involved in certain activities because we are committed first to our church family. One of the biggest battles we've encountered with our six-year-old has been over sporting events on Sunday. We've repeatedly had the discussion about why some of his friends can choose sports over attending church. We continually return to an eternal perspective and what matters most. We remind him of the priorities we have in place in our lives. As an adult, what are some things you may need to give up in order to give priority to your church family or service within the community? If you have children, how can you also guide them to do the same?

Service Projects

Some days, service projects simply involve sharing Jesus with someone who is lost in our community by providing them with a service, a snack, a gift, a meal, or some help on a specific project. Other days, this looks like a church-wide event of bringing a large meal to a fire station, cleaning small business bathrooms, or providing coffee and donuts to our hard working public servants.

Consider your own community. What are some of the greatest needs in your community, or even among your friends, that could use your assistance? How can you help in this way? Could you create a team of volunteers to serve together? Ask how you could be of service. We have done several surveys in our community and asked about some of the greatest needs in our area. We've come to realize that the major underlying need is a sense of purpose. Purpose gives people a reason to help others, to make big changes, to give up some of their comforts for the greater good of the people around them. Purpose is what ties communities together and changes cities for the Kingdom. Let's be the change in our community that gives people a purpose beyond themselves. How can you, as an individual, develop a team approach to serving others and advancing the Kingdom?

_____

_____

_____

_____

_____

_____

Family Serves **TOGETHER**

Together is what is most important. Yes, I could teach our children that Daddy is a pastor and so that's what he does to serve, but, in all actuality, God has called us all to serve together as the church. This means bringing our kids along for this wonderful and exhausting ride! If you are a parent, what are some ways you can encourage and even thrive in this area? How can you approach ministry as a family effort rather than reserved for certain adults or those in "leadership"? According to the Bible, we are all called to serve and be "doers of the Word." Consider some ways that you can be a "doer of the Word" in your own community.

Put People You are Already Serving in Your Kids' Lives

This may be a crazy idea to consider since we often like to protect our kids from heartache, hurt, or sin, but consider this: your children see it in the world every single day. But if they witness this brokenness and pain with you present to walk beside them, how much more will they comprehend the need for a Savior?

And how much more prepared will they be to face this dark world? Now, this is not to say we don't have "safe" people and families surrounding them. Our children have close relationships with other families who are pursuing the very same values that we strive to cultivate within our kids. Many of these friends are already serving in ministry. Because we are a church planting family, we've developed relationships with other church planting families, as well as with those who serve within other church plants, established churches, or ministries. Our kids are surrounded by people who understand the difficulty that comes with this lifestyle. Having solid believers around them outside of our church family is healing for all of us because we can find rest and comfort in them. Our children will always know safe spaces and people who won't abandon them.

As an individual or as a family in ministry, consider some people in your life who may be sources of comfort for you. Who are the people you can rest with and enjoy the peace that comes with their company? We have met these people within our own community via different avenues. We've made efforts to reach out to people who are serving the Kingdom in a similar capacity and make it a priority to spend time with them. How can you do the same with people who are doing the same in your own city?

ALL YOUR MIGHT

_____

_____

_____

_____

_____

Now that you have thought through some of these examples, what are three ways your faith call can be displayed on a weekly basis?

_____

_____

_____

_____

_____

_____

Home

In our home, our first priority is Jesus and sharing Him with lost people. Sometimes, this means having to say "no" to what we want to do or have within the physical characteristics of our home.

Simple Living (Living to Afford It)

Simple living can look very different depending on who you ask, but for us, it means living to afford to stay in our place of ministry. We live in a city with a high cost of living compared to the places where we were raised. Because of this, we've had to make many sacrifices and alter our budget in ways we would not have had to if we were serving Jesus in another city. But He called us to *this* city, so we will do what is necessary in order to be here. For us, this means that I need to provide some type of income. This also means that we do not regularly purchase small things that add up, like unnecessary clothing, coffee, or toys. Minimalism is a concept that has intrigued many in my generation. My version of minimalism is putting faith at the centerpiece and the call as the simple idea that we follow. This is the filter we use when being minimalistic with our time, money, energy, and, most importantly, family.

All Boys in One Room

We have our three older boys in one room for now. And, at the time of writing this book, we are in the process of moving our fourth boy into the same room with the other three within the next few months, with a space for the youngest as well. This can be complicated in terms of fitting two sets of bunk beds into a small space and storing clothes, toys, and books, but it also creates a sense of community for them that I don't think would be achieved otherwise.

Short Sale Home

Because we are called to our city specifically, we bought a short sale home that was, at the time, the cheapest house in the city. We have invested a great deal of time, effort, and money into fixing it up. Michael, specifically, has dedicated time to projects within the house to make it a place where we can minister to others. But again, this all comes back to perspective, priorities, and the passion behind it.

Simple Living for You:

What are some specific ways you can use these ideas to begin the simple living process within your own home? Simple living looks different for different homes and families, and I want you to think about the ways you can change the processes within your home. How can you open it up to be used by God in a more purposeful way? You may live in a city where you can more easily afford a larger home and use it in a different way than we use ours. What would it take for your home to become a place where you can regularly invite others in? You may have older children with friends from families who don't know Jesus. What would it take for your home to become a place where these youth enjoy coming for fun and to learn about a loving Christian family? You, too, may be on a very tight budget and be wondering how you could ever host people from your church or community while dealing with the financial strain of it?

These are all similar questions I have had and continue to have as we pursue this faith journey. I often want to close my family in and use the little money or space we have for my family alone. But it is all about purpose. And much hospitality can be extended, even on a very tight budget. You can have a home that is a welcoming space at 600 square feet and at 3000 square feet, with very little extra money or with an abundance.

> *Much Hospitality Can Be Extended* **EVEN ON A VERY TIGHT BUDGET.**

ALL YOUR MIGHT

One of the specific ways we welcome those in our community and church is by hosting a potluck. Each family attending is responsible for a different part of the meal, so it does not fall entirely to us. When we were living in a 640 square foot home, we'd still invited people to our home. We would gather the adults around the kitchen table for a game night, or in chairs or on the floor in our mini-family room for conversation and Bible study. Think through some of the aspects of your home and how it could be used to invite others in. Are you a great cook with a little extra spending money? Have one family over every week or so for a meal. Do you love to play games? Host a youth game night in your family room and make Bible study a part of it. Think through some of these options now as you consider the next question.

How can your faith call be displayed within your home?

_____

_____

_____

_____

_____

_____

Chase Your Faith:

Now that you've considered some of the ways your faith call can be displayed within your daily life, on a weekly basis, and within your home, consider how you can begin making these changes this week? Start small and build momentum. What is one idea you will implement in these three areas to change the trajectory of your faith journey now?

CHAPTER EIGHT

Big Faith, Bigger God

> *"We have no right to decide where we should be placed, or to have preconceived ideas as to what God is preparing for us to do. God engineers everything; and wherever He places us, our one supreme goal should be to pour out our lives in wholehearted devotion to Him in that particular work."*
> —Oswald Chambers

ON SEPTEMBER 29TH, 2015, MY incredible friend Brittany had three little boys three years old and under, a thriving ministry to women, many friends, and she loved the Lord with everything in her. But that morning, in one devastating blow, she lost her greatest earthly treasure: her husband. It was sudden and unexpected. Her whole world shook. And all who knew her watched.

How would she react? Would this break her? Her shocked family and friends, and even her entire city were watching her. On her blog, she wrote, "Through this journey God has been so faithful to us and it is my desire to use this pain for His mighty purpose. I have learned that even in the darkest places there is always HOPE in Christ and I love to share His hope with others."[6]

As I've watched her story unfold since that tragic day, I've found that it is through the small steps of faith she has been required to take each day that she now has a great influence of faith on the world.

God's Adventures are the Best Adventures

A dear mentor of mine shared the Chambers quote at the beginning of this chapter with me recently, and it has cut me to the core. Oh, to have such complete devotion to our Savior that we would, essentially, give up our preconceived ideas about what we should be doing and turn every area of our lives over to Him! You, dear one of faith, have the opportunity to live out this wholehearted devotion in the particular work God has for you. You have the chance to weave it into the fabric of your being, to intertwine it into every relationship you have with other believers and every encounter you experience with lost individuals.

God's adventures are the best adventures. Often, in the middle of hard places within our faith walk, it is hard to shout this from the rooftops. But if we quietly acknowledge it within our souls, we carve it on our hearts so that we can live in this knowledge and enjoy the journey. This is exactly the purpose of this chapter: to acknowledge that, while living out big faith is hard and monumental, God is also far greater and allows us to actually enjoy it.

Big faith must always be greater than our selfish desires. There is no way around it. Our comfort must never compete with the call of God when making a faith decision. As a believer, a faith decision should be the only type of decision we make.

Big Faith **MUST ALWAYS BE GREATER THAN OUR SELFISH DESIRES.**

When you feel God asking you to take a step within your job, your ministry, your home life, your family life, your community, or in any area of your life, you will need to take some vital steps to best determine the answer. As promised in Chapter Two, let's dig in a little deeper to the idea of a Faith Challenge.

The Faith Challenge is:

- ❏ Pray and ask God to help you determine your faith step. Continue praying about that specific step at least once a day.
- ❏ Read Scripture related to the step.
- ❏ Find a mentor and an accountability partner.
- ❏ If married, have continual conversations with your spouse about the faith step.
- ❏ Fast at least once during the determination process.
- ❏ Never allow money to determine the decision.
- ❏ Once determined, burn the ships!

Let's look at each step. Take the opportunity to work through some of these steps that you can apply every time you are facing a new faith journey, or even a smaller faith step, in your life.

Prayer

I know that this is often spoken about, but it is not taken as seriously as it should be. Prayer will be the most important part of your faith journey. It's that simple and that important. You must pursue God's will in daily, consistent prayer. So much prayer in so many moments, every day. It is the way for our eyes to be opened to the work God is doing in our lives. Philippians 4:6 allows us to find rest in the power of prayer: "Do not be anxious about anything, but in every situation, by prayer and petition, with thanksgiving, present your requests to God."

Jeremiah 29:12 also encourages us by stating, "Then you will call on me and come and pray to me, and I will listen to you."

Great men and women of faith only accomplished big goals from the Lord by following through in deep and consistent prayer. Jerry Falwell shared about the time he was in his Bible college and asked to use an empty dorm room for prayer. Every day, we went in the room to pray in silence for several hours. He petitioned God for the hearts of the young boys who were coming to his Bible study and asked for a move from God. In return, God performed a great deal of miracles through him. A. T. Pierson once said, "There has never been a spiritual awakening in any country or locality that did not begin in united prayer."

Now, as busy men and women with careers, stay-at-home moms, college students, or older men and women with families or health concerns, it might not be possible to spend most of your day in an empty dorm room, pouring your heart out to God. But what are some ways you can seek God in prayer in the midst of the busyness surrounding you? How can you find moments in your life where God is the center of your attention? In my life, this looks like taking one or two minutes throughout the day and sharing a worry or a need with God. It looks like praying before my feet hit the floor in the morning, even if only for a moment. It looks like reaching out to friends with prayer requests so I know that more people are bring that request before the Lord. It looks like praying with my children before each meal and before bed. It looks like spending just a few minutes in prayer when we see or hear of an accident. Often, when crying out to God for a specific need for those in our community or within our church, it means giving up some of our own leisure time. It may mean skipping our favorite show, a book, working out, or the usual rest time we have during kids' nap times or even sleep at night to devote several hours to prayer. If we make prayer a priority, we will fit it in, regardless of any obstacles or excuses. Think through your schedule now. How could you devote just five more minutes of your day to prayer?

> IF WE *Make Prayer a Priority,* WE WILL FIT IT IN, REGARDLESS OF ANY OBSTACLES OR EXCUSES.

Scripture

Of course, turning to Scripture is vital when making a major decision. But how can we specifically do this as it relates to determining your specific faith step? Have a Bible reading plan. I recommend the Life Journal[7] and the SOAP method. The Life Journal will keep you on track for reading the Bible on a daily basis for a year. The SOAP method stands for Scripture, Observation, Application, and Prayer. This is an effective tool for your daily quiet time. I use the Bible Reading Plan found within the Life Journal to determine what to read each day. You could use this plan or another Bible reading plan. There are also some great plans on the YouVersion Bible App.

After completing your reading, choose a verse or a few verses that stood out to you during your reading. Write down what you observed about the verse or verses that struck you. Then, write down how it can be applied to your personal life today. Finally, write a prayer to God about what you learned and ask for His help in applying it to your life.

It's a simple process, but one that enables you to draw more from your daily Scripture reading. I use the *Life Journal* to complete the SOAP method as well as the actual Bible reading plan.

Additionally, be sure to look up specific passages of Scripture related to faith, and follow Paul's missionary journeys in Acts 13-

14, Acts 15-18, and Acts 18-20. Often, these will speak to you about your present situation.

Mentor Insight and Accountability

I can't recommend mentorship and accountability enough. The other night, my husband and I were talking about the mentors we've had in our lives and the incredible encouragement and advice they've offered over the years. We both confirmed that we wouldn't be where we are today without them. We have some God-fearing individuals in our lives who have walked His path so well before us and can offer more wisdom than any peer ever could. We have often found that our generation seeks out peer influence and advice when making big faith decisions, but peers can only offer it from their similar, limited perspective. But someone who has already been there and walked the path can see things far more clearly.

> SOMEONE WHO HAS ALREADY BEEN THERE AND WALKED THE PATH CAN SEE THINGS *Far More Clearly*

Do that this week. Find someone in your life who you trust, admire, feel encouraged by, who follows Jesus with their whole heart, who has made big leaps of faith, and who has followed through on them. Concerning the specific process of finding a mentor, consider your area of ministry. Are you a ministry wife, an elder, a father, a mother, a college student, a career-oriented person, someone in retirement? No matter where you are in life, there is someone who can mentor you.

Are you hoping to be a better leader and desire to succeed more in a specific area? Consider the people in your life. Do you have solid faith leaders within your community? Do you have friends with incredible mentors who are influencing their lives? Could you reach out to these friends for some recommendations from their mentors?

The mentors in my life have generally come from the churches I've been a part of, but it could be someone within another church in your community as well. As a pastor's wife, for me, it is often the wives of pastors my husband respected and admired. I wanted to learn everything I could from these women who were doing the same thing I had found myself doing for my husband in ministry.

If you want to be a better wife, seek out a woman who is being that for her husband. If you want to be a better husband, seek out a godly man to emulate. If you want to be a better elder or leader, seek out someone within your own church, family, or community that is serving well in this same way. If you want to be a better college student or career person for the Lord, look for someone who is making a difference for Jesus in the current marketplace while also being successful at the work they have set out to do. If you are in retirement, look for someone who has used this time for the Lord and who can guide you on this path. The best way to choose who you would like to mentor you is by observing someone who displays the qualities you would like to strengthen in your own life. If you would like to be a better steward of your time, find someone who is doing this for the glory of the Kingdom. Consider yourself and your strengths and weakness. What are some strengths you would like to make stronger and what are your weaknesses you would like to improve? Another option is to ask your loved ones who may be good people to reach out to in this area. I have often found myself asking my husband for advice when it comes to mentorship.

Once you have determined one or two people who could be excellent mentors for you, you may feel a bit uncomfortable reaching out and asking them to mentor you. This can feel awkward; however, in my experience, the people I have asked to mentor me have felt nothing but honor and gratitude: grateful they were asked and honored to do it. The way I have approached this is by highlighting the areas of their life I would like to emulate and the areas in my life I would like to strengthen. Depending on the person I have asked, the mentoring process looks a bit different. I have met with mentors on a regular basis (weekly, bi-weekly, monthly) as well as only when I had specific concerns or questions. As a mentor myself, I have done the same depending on the individual. I believe this process is fluid and speaking with your chosen mentor about expectations is the best approach. If you desire to be more like them in the area of spirituality and Bible knowledge, consider meeting for a study for a specific length of time. If you desire better time management skills, simply observing them as they live life may be the best option.

After you have reached out to your chosen mentor, have a conversation about what will work best for the two of you and that relationship. If, for some reason, your chosen mentor lets you know that they are unable to fulfill this role, it's ok! I have had this happen before and even after the mentoring relationship began. While this is disappointing, it is best to know and to find a more fulfilling mentoring relationship for both parties in the future. Just begin the process over again to determine a better fit for you. Below, list a few people you might consider to be mentors. Think and pray about these names and then reach out to one (or more!).

Conversations with Your Spouse

If you are married, I pray you have already had the conversation concerning the faith step by this point. Not only is it important to have conversations together, but to also have conversations with God together. Jesus is the ultimate facilitator and He can change hearts like no one else. Come together and follow Him wholeheartedly. Often, this does not feel like this can be the case when your spouse is not on board with the faith step or when you feel like you're hearing conflicting things from the Lord. This has been a concern I have seen both within my personal life as well as the lives of many women I've known (and I am sure it is the same for men).

Because the Bible discusses at great length the idea of two becoming one, I would be hesitant to make any large faith step apart from your spouse; however, when it comes to being obedient to the Lord or not, this is a major concern that should be addressed. For example, I know several women whose husbands do not attend church with them and several women who have chosen not to attend church because of their husband's refusal to go. When it comes to this small step of obedience to God that is not life-altering to the marriage, it is vital that the individual follows God first and foremost, while still being respectful to their spouse. When it comes to a major decision concerning a faith step that may include a move or another major change, it is important to come together, pray, fast, and discuss it together until you can come to a place of agreement about God's call on your life.

For me, the call to go to Raleigh is one that Michael clearly heard from God and one that I did not. We were in a good place in Georgia, surrounded by good friends, a great church family, and a city that I loved. Now, I realized that we couldn't continue living there and it was time to actually step out on our own in ministry. I recognized that my husband had a desire to go to seminary. However, in my mind, there were much easier options for this desire that included a salary while he was in seminary. He had received another viable option that, to me, seemed much more appropriate for where we were in life. My husband understood this and spoke with several mentors about the desire of his heart. He wanted to be sure that this was from God and not only from himself. He had a mentor mention to him that, if he wanted to be a church planter eventually, why not begin that process now while he was in seminary? While that made sense to both of us, it was still scary to process. But often, God will ask you to say "yes" to one thing when he really wants you to say "yes" to another. God was asking us to say "yes" to seminary, which was in the Raleigh area, just to get us to say "yes" to serving in Raleigh. As a couple, we came together and prayed about it, discussed conversations we had with our mentors, sought the Scriptures, and really hashed out our concerns over this decision. In the end, I understand where God was leading us; however, even if I hadn't, God has given my husband the role of the spiritual leader within our house and I respect that role.

The discussion of a submissive wife in Ephesians 5:22-33 often causes great anger and misunderstanding in our society today; how-ever, many people miss the second part of that passage, which commands husbands to love their wives even *as Christ loved the church* and gave Himself up for her. This is a major commandment and one that is even harder to execute, in my opinion, than simply being submissive to a godly husband. It requires that a husband must love his wife in a way that is nearly impossible. And he can only do this with an incredibly close relationship with the Father. Having this incredibly close relationship with the Father means I can trust my husband's lead.

> HAVING A CLOSE RELATIONSHIP WITH THE FATHER MEANS *I Can Trust My Husband's Lead.*

More Prayer and Fasting

Along with prayer comes fasting. For any big faith decision we've made, fasting has been a priority. Even in our call to plant a church in Montana, we committed to a 40-day fast from all meat and dairy (two very hard food types for us to give up). It was only through the commitment of the 40-day fast that God revealed Montana as a plan for our lives. Fasting is humbling. It brings you to your knees. It enables you to listen for and consider His will more throughout the day. You can fast from a large variety of desires or needs in your life. It may not even be related to food. I have often fasted from social media, the use of my phone, or favorite activities that have distracted me from seeking God's will in a specific area of my life. Fasting helps us pare down to the minimum in life so that we can seek God out with more focus and attention. This may look very different for each of us, but should play a major role within decision-making concerning faith steps.

Never Allow Money to Determine the Decision

We've heard from people, time and time again, that they have made a faith decision based on the salary or financial benefit that accompanied it.

Never let money determine how you follow God. This is a difficult topic to discuss, and one that offends many people, so I tread lightly here. It is also difficult because it is an area of control for us as human beings.

Never Let Money Determine
HOW YOU FOLLOW GOD.

Money is security and taking a faith step in this area requires leaving our comfort zone and place of safety to fully take advantage of the actual freedom that comes with it.

As a self-proclaimed worrier, I get it. I *completely* get it. There is a balance in this area when it comes to being wise with our money, taking care of our loved ones, and stewarding our finances well. Let's dance this fine line and discover how to handle it in our current day and age.

First, we need to adjust our perspective. If we have the perspective that all of our money is given to us by God and is ultimately *His* money, then we don't view it in the same way as before. Second, if we remember that our families are given to us by God, and that He cares for them even more than we do, we grow in trust and confidence in God. Third, if we are in constant communication with God throughout our day, every single financial decision, no matter how small, is run through the filter of God's ultimate authority in our lives.

Of course, you and I both know this is not easy. Personally, we are steeped in financial concerns due to student loans from college (an investment, but a stressor none the less). We have many children who rely on us for their needs. We desire to travel to see our families who live far away. We've also battled health issues, surgeries, and other therapies. All of these take a financial toll. But we must remember the end goal of the race. Then, we are able to pass these concerns to the Lord and be willing to follow, no matter the financial cost. The best way to achieve this freedom is through continual prayer and remembrance of our purpose.

Let Immediate Family Know, Including Children

If you do have children that are old enough to understand, they should be the first to know once your faith step is determined. Then, include your extended family in this journey, sharing with them your vision. If they are believers, ask them to pray for you in this step.

Go and Burn the Ships!

In 1519, Captain Hernan Cortes landed in Veracruz to begin his great conquest. Upon arriving, he ordered his men to burn the ships! Steven Curtis Chapman wrote a song about this historical event. It was a favorite of mine as a child and continues to hold true in my adult life:

> *"Quietly they whispered, "Let's sail back to the life we knew"*
> *But the one who led them there was saying*
> *"Burn the ships we're here to stay*

There's no way we could go back
Now that we've come this far by faith
Burn the ships we've passed the point of no return
Our life is here so let the ships burn."

Man or woman of faith, I am preaching to myself as I share this. I have so often doubted my ministry, my call, many faith steps, and have even told my husband it's time to retreat. But here's the thing: retreat is easy when you have the option to do so. We have given so much over to God with our faith step to church plant in Montana. All of our mentors, great men and women of God, have invested in us through prayer, financial partnership, mission work, and in so many other ways, that retreat is just not an option. We will succeed or die trying unless God pursues our hearts for a completely different path that He, and only He, has chosen for us.

After we've taken our step of faith, which could be a specific location we're called to, a ministry we've entered, a selfish pursuit we've given up, or anything and everything in between, and, in doing so, burned the ships, how are our families affected? In a previous chapter, I spoke of my desire to start a conference for teenage girls. Teen girls have always been the passion of my heart, and I still work very closely with many in my area. I do this through mentoring relationships, by hosting events at our church, and by teaching them. However, God called us to church planting when we were first married. He knit it into every part of our being as a couple. I then had to let God's plan for my life overrule the specific plan I had for myself as an individual in ministry. Giving up a selfish pursuit of something doesn't always mean that it is a bad thing or even hurtful. It means that we turn our lives over to God and, essentially, don't look back. I still believe that one day I will have an even bigger ministry to teen girls and reach even more young ladies in places outside the U.S. for God's Kingdom. But when we said "yes" to His desire for us to plant a church in Montana, we made ourselves an offering. This means that I have been serving in kids' ministry, an area I never envisioned myself prior to this process.

What does this look like for you? Your "burning the ships" moment may not be related to any type of ministry opportunity. For me, it was because my ministry to God is who I am as a person and individual and affects me deeply; but for you, it might mean giving up specific career goals to further the Gospel, or giving up wants that you have to start a family, or taking time to invest in another person and therefore giving up the little time you have to yourself. Think on this and, even when it sounds ludicrous, know that having a "burn the ships" moment is one of the most freeing things you can do!

Priority Management

We must keep our priorities in this very specific order:

- ❏ God
- ❏ Spouse
- ❏ Immediate family, including children
- ❏ Others

If we do not continue to value our direct relationship with the Father who brought us to this place, we will lose sight of why we are created to be here on this earth. Our purpose can only be found in a daily relationship with our Abba Daddy, our Great Counselor, the King who rules and guides everything in the world and everything in our life and journey.

And of course, if you are married, you must cling to your spouse. You have to agree, you have to be a team, and you must maintain the mentality that it is "us" together to face a world that the enemy is working to destroy. Remember, that devil fights hard. Know that, as a married couple serving God together, your marriage will be attacked, even more than if you hadn't followed your calling as a team. The wiles of the devil are no joke in the spiritual battleground of ministry, specifically in marriages devoted to ministry. One of the best and most practical ways to combat the attacks of the devil is to recognize him for who he is, both in your own soul and within your marriage. In his book *Crash the Chatterbox*, Steven Furtick talks about this in great detail. He discusses the chatter that is constantly taking place in our minds and hearts. This chatter is directly conducted by Satan with the goal of making you feel alone in this battle. He'll do it within your own person, damaging your self-esteem and attitude. And he'll hit your marriage hard. You'll find yourself tempted to question your spouse, their motives, their love for you, their decisions, and their leadership. Furtick says, "The more you grow in Christ and the closer you get to fulfilling the things He put you on the earth to do, the more intense the battle with your chatter becomes."[8] He also mentions that God is the one who convicts, while Satan is the one who condemns. To fully recognize Satan, we must recognize him for who he is, a condemner and an accuser. My husband once shared in a sermon, "If the devil can keep you accused, he can keep you unused." Isn't this the truth? He will keep you unused in your personal spiritual walk with God, in your marriage, in your job, and in your ministry. The way I remind myself of the truth is by going directly to the source of truth. I know that Satan leaves me feeling worthless, but I know that the Holy Spirit spurs me on toward my purpose.

> *God Is the One Who Convicts,* WHILE SATAN IS THE ONE WHO CONDEMNS.

One of the ways that we include our children in big faith decisions is by sharing it with them in an exciting way once we've fully understood God's calling and solidified the big changes that will need to be made. Our children are young right now, so I can't pretend to understand the struggles that come with parenting teenagers through a big faith step, but I can relate to the experiences I endured as a teenager making big faith moves with my family. Knowing the reasons behind the faith step and what it would look like when we were on the journey, and how much prayer and guidance from God and other mentors was involved, made all the difference. Once they are included on the ride, we have to be open to regular and consistent conversations about the shift. Following Jesus with reckless abandon is hard, and they endure just as much as we do when living out our faith in a way the enemy hates.

Managing a faith life totally devoted to the call of God is not easily managed with five young children, and I won't promise you won't experience some of the same difficulties. We have to keep our kids abreast of what God is asking us without scarring them by some of the painful experiences we encounter. Some days I succeed. Other days, I completely drop the ball. What I've learned is it has to be "us" together in ministry, not only my husband and me with our children simply tagging along. Even as little unbelievers who don't yet have a personal relationship with Jesus, they're learning what it means to serve others. Eventually, when the passion and fire consume them, they'll know what living out their faith by loving others looks like as they've been learning from us since day one. Just the other day, while we were driving, my oldest said to my second, "Mommy and Daddy are here in Bozeman, but I wonder where God will ask us to go one day?" They already understand that life is about where God calls, not where we feel most comfortable. I only pray that their hearts will continue to be open to the will of God.

Ministry to others comes after relationships within our immediate family, but it is still one of the top four priorities in our life. All facets of a life of ministry must fall within the guidelines of the Great Commission: "Therefore go and make disciples of all nations, baptizing them in the name of the Father and of the Son and of the Holy Spirit, and teaching them to obey everything I have commanded you. And surely I am with you always, to the very end of the age." (Matthew 28:19-20). So the primary goal within ministry is to make disciples, and we do this by living our faith on a daily basis, even when the going is slow or frustrating. In *Purpose Driven Church*, Rick Warren says: "Spiritual maturity is demonstrated more by behavior than by beliefs."[9] Isn't this the truth? We show our growth in maturity by how we live out the commands, by how we display the Great Commission for the whole world to see, and, ultimately, by our behavior rather than what we know to be Truth. The Great Commission compels us to make disciples, baptize them, and teach them to observe God's commands in the Bible.

Once we've determined the steps we are supposed to take and where we are supposed to go (or stay), we have to take the time to rest and abide in the peace God offers. You will have days when you wonder, "What have I done? Was I really following God to come here or start this or stay here or share this?"

REMEMBER AND Find Rest.

But, always, *always* go back to your call. Remember and find rest.

Lastly, the most important aspect of your faith journey is to enjoy it! Have fun living the adventure! You have to extend grace to yourself and your family. You cannot be everything to everyone, but you can be exactly who God has designed you to be. And you can have fun while doing it!

Chase Your Faith:

How are your priorities being lived out on a daily basis? What are some changes you can make this week so that the priorities of your life line up with God's best for you?

What are some ways you can use the Faith Challenge with a faith step you are facing right now? How will you incorporate each of these steps into your life?

CHAPTER NINE

Lions for Jesus

The wicked run away when no one is chasing them, but the godly are as bold as lions.
— *Proverbs 28:1*

WHEN I WAS NEARLY NINETEEN years old, I met Michael's family for the first time. As I sat around their kitchen table surrounded with both sets of his grandparents, his parents, and his siblings, I shared the meaning of my name and why my parents chose it. They were astounded to learn that my name means "Lion of God" in Hebrew, and not just because of the big meaning. You see, when my mother-in-law first started having children, she prayed that they would be lions for Jesus in all that they set out to do for the Lord. To discover that she had prayed for her children to be the very same thing my name meant was a reassuring whisper from the Lord.

Boldly Led

I often think about that day and how God granted me peace in that moment. Michael and I were not in a relationship yet, but it enabled me to trust the journey. Knowing that my future spouse had been prayed for in the same specific way my parents had claimed me from birth meant even more as the years passed.

Now, I can't help but pray boldly over my children's lives. I pray that they will be able to loudly proclaim the Gospel wherever God calls them to as children and, one day, as adults. I want to raise little missionaries who are lions for Jesus, untouched by the casualties that will inevitably come with ministry and service to others.

Statistics show that 85% of American believers became Christians between the ages of four and fourteen.[10] Wow. As a parent with incredible influence over my children, this is sobering. Statistics also show that 70% of young adults who regularly attended church for at least one year during high school left the church upon graduation.[11]

Our society has created a phenomenon that enables parents to seek out a lifestyle for their children that is depriving them of the most important character qualities they need to thrive as adults. Have we, as Christian parents, committed ourselves to pursuing a lifestyle that our world perpetuates as the best, while giving up the most important attributes that enable our children to be healthy and Godly human beings in adulthood? We trade humility for getting ahead no matter what. We trade crucial time together for countless extracurricular activities. We trade a desire for God's will for a desire for what our families or society expect. We trade the freedom that comes with giving our lives in complete devotion to Christ for a more popular opinion of ourselves in peer groups. We trade using our gifts and talents in service to our Father for the use of them in a world that doesn't recognize or value them. We trade our children's tender hearts for the Gospel for other unimportant tasks. In every area of our life, there is a trade happening. We have to recognize if we are actually trading the good for something worse.

We want to be a family who does real ministry together. The kind of ministry that is often difficult, behind the scenes, and unappreciated. The kind of ministry that requires acknowledgement solely from God to keep going, as that is often the only voice encouraging us. I want my kids to know that it's all about *Him* and never about *us*.

Rearing Lions

So what does this approach look like? First of all, we include the kids in all areas of service. We want their heartbeat to be loving God and loving people, even when it's downright messy. Our oldest two beg to set up at church with their dad, often leaving the house before 7 a.m. They help with tear down at church, get our house ready for Life Group or other guests, help prepare for our kids ministry on a very regular basis, and help with any other service projects or events we may have. There are three core values I pray are instilled in them as children that they can carry into adulthood. These core values will offer them guidance in any area they choose to work or serve:

- Ministry over laziness
- Following God's call over allowing extravagance
- Putting others over self

These three areas serve three separate character qualities: hard work ethic, simple faith, and selflessness.

So how can we, as parents, instill these things in ourselves on a daily basis? And how can we instill these things in our children?

First, let's be held accountable. Set a deadline for yourself. By the end of this week, your goal is to find someone in your life who you trust and who you know will actually hold you accountable to adhering to these three things in your life. For me, I have several accountability partners who do this, one of whom is another church planter's wife. She knows that these are things we both face on a daily basis, and I constantly reach out to her. Some days, it's a quick text asking how she is doing and filling her in about my heart and life. Other days, it's a lengthy phone call where we hash out some of our next steps for both our personal lives and our lives in ministry. Our relationship includes advice, encouragement, and, sometimes, a swift kick in the pants to remind each other to get back on for the ride. She knows the dead parts that God is working to prune within my soul and she encourages me in these areas.

Second, let's talk with our kids about these qualities and what they look like in our homes, our churches, our work, and our schools. Let's open this conversation while we're driving in the car, waiting on a family member to get ready, and eating at the dinner table. My personal goal is to talk about one of these three areas at every meal. Let's make the most use of our time together. After all, we have very little time at home with our children in the course of their lifetime.

Third, take action. We can only do so much talking before it must become an overflow of our heart. We must lead by example. Get your family to church on a regular basis. Regularly does not mean when there is nothing better to do. Regularly means that it is a priority in your lives and that you are making it a priority in your children's lives. Let them see what a body of believers working together to serve God looks like.

Finally, don't simply be a watching member of the church, encouraging your children to do the same. This will only teach them that the church is all about what they can *receive* from it. Be a participant. Serve, love, give! Of course, you can do this outside the church as well, but starting within the church body is a great place to build a foundation with the necessary resources. Talk to your pastor, your ministry leaders, and your children's ministry about ways you can be involved. Then, talk to them about how your kids can serve, too. Right now, I am not serving in an area that I am particularly passionate about, but it is exactly where God wants me. Is this frustrating when I see others neglecting to serve? Of course. But we are called to serve God where we are planted. Our focus must be on serving Him or else we'll become discouraged. People will disappoint us, but serving God is the ultimate goal.

OUR FOCUS MUST BE ON *Serving Him* OR ELSE WE'LL BECOME DISCOURAGED.

Lion Trainers

My kids do things that most parents would never dream their kids could do! Does this mean they're somehow better? Absolutely not! It means we have put expectations on them that even the Lord defends in the Bible. We read in Paul's letter to Timothy, "Don't let anyone look down on you because you are young, but set an example for the believers in speech, in conduct, in love, in faith and in purity" (1 Timothy 4:12). The Bible claims that faith and ministry are not just for the few, but for all, even the youngest ones. Ecclesiastes 12:1 also reiterates this idea by stating, "Remember your Creator in the days of your youth, before the days of trouble come and the years approach when you will say, "I find no pleasure in them."" And in Jeremiah 1:7-9, we are reminded that the youth of our children is no excuse for disobeying God's commands: "But the Lord said to me, "Do not say, 'I am too young.' You must go to everyone I send you to and say whatever I command you. Do not be afraid of them, for I am with you and will rescue you," declares the Lord."

One of the best parts about our story is that our children have experienced what very few are able to by being a part of a larger purpose. They have ventured forward in faith, along with us, before they even truly knew what faith means. This is not to say we haven't had our challenges with the balance of determining when it is too much. This is something we have been and are still learning day by day.

As a parent, how can you best handle this in your current circumstances? What are some ways you can make some changes to your daily and weekly schedule to ensure that your children are living for the Lord and not for themselves? Do you have specific concerns about instituting this if they are heavily involved in sports or other extracurricular activities? I have often found that many parents do feel the need to cut back in these areas, but don't know where to start. Or, they haven't even considered it because it's just how it is for our American culture. I've always hated the term "balance" because life isn't about "balance."

> *It's about Giving Priority TO SPECIFIC AREAS OF OUR LIVES AND LESS PRIORITY TO OTHERS.*

Rather, it's about giving priority to specific areas of our lives and less priority to others. This is not a balancing act.

As an individual, consider the very specific priorities in your life in order of their value. Then, sit down, as parents, and hash out some of the priorities you envision for your family. Finally, bring your family together and discuss the priorities you have as a family and how these will play out in your lives. Yes, there should be room in your life for activities, leisure, and involvement within the community, but there must be a specific purpose behind everything that is chosen to be a part of your life. Can your children live out God's call for their lives within the sports arena or after-school activities? Absolutely. Should it interfere with the more important aspects of faith, fellowship with believers, and following God's will? Absolutely not. That is the key. Determine how these things fit in your family life under the top priorities of time with God, time with your family, sharing the Gospel, and ministry.

We want to raise our children to be faithful, not just busy. Our kids are happiest and most fulfilled when we're living out our purpose. It gives them a confidence that they cannot find in anything else. As David wrote in the Psalms, "For you have been my hope, Sovereign Lord, my confidence since my youth!" (Psalm 71:5). You may not know where God wants you or your family to serve until you start diving in and helping where you are needed. So please, for the love, don't just wait on someone to approach you. Ask around and be the hands and feet of Jesus!

> **WE WANT TO RAISE OUR CHILDREN TO BE FAITHFUL. *Not Just Busy.***

Chase Your Faith:

What are some specific changes you can make in your family life now that will take your children from being busy to being faithful?

_____

_____

_____

_____

_____

How can you personally implement the 3 core values mentioned above to be more purposeful in your parenting?

_____

_____

_____

_____

_____

_____

CHAPTER TEN

Put Your Money Where Your Mouth Is

> *"As James Adams was coining the phrase "American Dream", Franklin Roosevelt was emphasizing how Americans will postpone immediate gratification and even endure hard sacrifices if they are convinced their future will be better than their past."*
>
> —David Platt in Radical

DURING THE FIRST YEAR OF our marriage, we made a combined income of about $10,000. Because of my husband's leadership and guidance during that year, we still tithed at least the full 10% every month. In years following, when we also made very little, we still continued to tithe at least 10% as well. In 2010, my husband was serving as a mentee under Dr.

Johnny Hunt at First Baptist Woodstock. Pastor Johnny offered Michael and me so much guidance over the years, but one area that has forever changed me is his very generous heart. He gives away more of what he earns than he keeps. When we asked him about this area of his life, he told us that if you're not generous when you have very little income, you will never be generous when you have much. While this is something we've heard hundreds of times, and even read about in the Bible with the widow's offering, it puts it in a totally different perspective when we look at it in terms of individual lives in today's world.

The Cost of the Kingdom

Here's some real data about the devastating reality of giving in today's world:

- Tithers make up only 10-25 percent of a normal congregation.

- Only 5% of the U.S. tithes, with 80% of Americans only giving 2% of their income.

- Christians are only giving at 2.5% per capita, while during the Great Depression, they gave at a 3.3% rate.[12]

Always, always, always choose faith over a false sense of security. Your real security is in the One who cares more about you than anything else in creation. As a student at Liberty University, I often heard Jerry Falwell speak about BHAGS, or Big Hairy Audacious Goals. He had so many BHAGS in his life in which he didn't take money into consideration as much as others would have desired. Choosing his faith in what God could do over the financial worry often cost him a good bit when it all panned out, but resulted in BIG results for the Kingdom. He taught me that God calls us to BHAGS all the time, and that a selfish fear of losing financial security can be detrimental. Had he not followed his BHAGS, my alma mater wouldn't exist. So many of us pursue career goals and financial goals as the *ultimate* goals in our lives. If someone were to ask you what your biggest goals for your life and family are, what would you say? Many of us would talk about our goal for the professional position we'd like, or how financially secure we'd like to be, or what education we'd like to obtain. Have you considered a goal of working hard enough to be able to give most of your money away? Or trusting the Lord enough to venture to the most obscure places no matter the outcome?

Always Choose Faith OVER A FALSE SENSE OF SECURITY.

No matter where we're called geographically, it is always about the ministry God has designed specifically for us, and never about the money. We've heard students fresh out of college or seminary discuss how they'll choose their ministry job based on the salary. This principle even applies to those in a secular job because we are *all* in ministry. As vessels of the one King who knows what is best for our lives, we cannot accept a position simply for the money it offers. On the contrary, we have to dig deep, pray hard, and determine in faith where God would have us go.

In our faith journey, one of the choices we've made is to never take a job based on the salary. If we did, the decision would be based on our own wants and desires and *not* based on where God wants us. Rather, we've chosen to filter every area of our lives through our call. We've chosen to set the things that matter to God as the things that matter to us. What matters to God is having us reach the people He has called us to reach. He loves people who have never been reached with the Gospel that only *you* can reach.

So, for us, this means putting our "yes" on the table despite the lack of "appropriate" income, even as a family of 7. We've also had to give up some things that others consider essential. We've given up the potential for a secure salary at an established church and have instead relied on friends, family, and partner churches to prayerfully support us each month. We've given up a specific retirement plan that a "normal" job may offer, pushing us to create our own. We've given up the ability for me to be a stay-at-home mom without the responsibility of providing income for our five children. And we've given up the security of having family close by for support and help with the children. We've given up the affordability of living in a place where the housing market isn't skyrocketing. And we give up other little securities on a daily basis.

Cashing Out

Look at your current financial life. What are some things you said you would never be able to give up that you really could, if only by your faith in God? What about your job? Is it where God has called you to be? Or your city? What in your life are you clinging to that God is asking you to release?

We do make investments in people in terms of our financial budget. This means paying for people to go to trainings, paying for materials to give to the lost or to those who come to our Life Group in our home, and giving away more of God's money that He's given to us to use for His glory, one person at a time.

We're also very minimalistic in what we give our kids. This helps us to keep our priorities in line, but it also helps them as well.

Like I mentioned before, our main goal is to help our children see their purpose in life and pursue it with fervor. Materialistically, this means that we have a very small section of a window bench in our house that contains all their toys. When this gets too full, we go through it together and determine what will be given away to other kids or sold so that they can purchase a book or game.

We don't deny our children their needs, but we help them focus their wants toward the good things in life and not toward the materialistic things that will never satisfy their deep desires. I think so many of us missed out on this lesson as children. So we talk about this perspective with our kids regularly. The very best way to actually teach your kids about minimalism is to model it on a daily basis and by answering their questions along the way.

Giving Back

An area that is an issue for so many is that of giving and tithing. This is as much a part of your faith life as every other area. It is a commandment from our God and it is one of the most valuable practices of our Christian life. It doesn't just impact us as individuals, but it changes the hearts of all those watching. And it makes a *huge* difference for the recipient.

PUT YOUR MONEY WHERE YOUR MOUTH IS

Rick Warren says: "Now the antidote to the lust of the eyes is generosity. Learning to be generous is the only antidote to the lust of the eyes."[13]

He tells a story about how he and his wife began giving to the church and how they made a decision at the beginning of their marriage to become more generous every year of their lives. They decided to raise their tithe each year. They started with 10% because that is what God commands, but each year they'd raise it a little bit more. Rick didn't tell anyone about this plan for thirty years. As of the time I heard this story, they had raised their tithe from 90% to 91%. He explained that God says to him, "You give to me and I'll give to you and we'll see who wins. I have lost that game every year for thirty-eight years." At this event, Rick dared the people present to trust God and claimed that if you don't trust God with your money, you don't trust Him. He had a decades-long track record of giving money to God, even when he didn't have it. And in turn, God trusted him with the best-selling book in American history. God knew what he'd do with the money. Luke 16:10-11 states, "Whoever can be trusted with very little can also be trusted with much, and whoever is dishonest with very little will also be

IF YOU DON'T TRUST GOD WITH YOUR MONEY, You Don't Trust Him.

dishonest with much. So if you have not been trustworthy in handling worldly wealth, who will trust you with true riches?" Finally, Rick challenges Christians everywhere by boldly proclaiming: "You can give without loving, but you can't love without giving." [14]

One way to step out in faith is to give God's money back to him via the church. While the word "tithe" actually means "tenth" and therefore a tenth of what you earn should be given back to God, there are many other ways to give within the church. Meet with your pastor or a staff member and develop a plan for ways you can bless your local community, state, or the world through missions beyond the four walls of your church. I can promise you, you will never regret giving more to advance the Kingdom.

As a family, we also do some giving beyond tithes to those people who are serving in the U.S. and overseas, and to others who are pursuing their calling or serving in other areas of ministry. If you would like to give in this way, my first recommendation is to find a church planter or a few church planters in your town. Call them or meet with them to "interview" them, making sure they align with you theologically. Don't let them know why you're doing it. Then, simply make an anonymous donation to them. Another option is to give to the North American Mission Board (NAMB), the International Mission Board (IMB,) or other church planting networks within your state or community. Prayerfully, you're going to a church that is planting other churches and focuses on this within their missions program. If that is the case, be sure to give to a specific church planting or missions fund through your own church. Your church may also have a strategic church partnership program. This would also be another way to give to another church through the church you attend. These are just some options we've used and are great ways to give beyond your tithes to your church.

As a family, we also invest in a good deal of supplies we use to help us serve and care for people. Some of these things include products for our meals together with other families, life group supplies, items needed for our children's ministries and youth ministry, and taking those who serve in our church out for meals. We always have some great Bibles on hand to give to those who need them, and we love to give away books and gift cards just to say "thank you" to those who serve with us. Laying down our lives in this way comes at a steeper cost to us with a husband in ministry, but it is in this daily sacrifice that we actually pick up our cross and follow Him.

Our specific faith journey even involves where we live. We have intentionally purchased our home as a space of ministry. In the very early days of our church plant, we met at our home as a small group, and having adequate space for parking and chairs in our living room has always been a key investment for us. Eventually, when we started our first preview services, they were also at our home in an original garage that we turned into a large room. Although we outgrew this space as a regular gathering space, we continue to use it for our life groups, youth events, kids ministry prep parties, appreciation events, and simply for having families over for dinner. People were often confused when we purchased our home in the more expensive city in our valley. But being in a place that was easily accessible, especially in the early days of our church, was a top priority. Even our oldest recently commented that we couldn't live in a house that he loved because it was far outside of town, "Then what would we do for Life Group?"

What does this look like for you? While you may not be a church planter, what does it mean to make large financial decisions, even in regards to your own home? Consider your home as an opportunity to use as a meeting space for your church, as a place to pour into and bless others, or as a safe haven for those who may need it. How can it be used in a more purposeful way?

A Lasting Legacy

Both my husband and I are often asked how our children handle this journey, especially in this area of financial faith. While we certainly do not have all the answers, I know that our biggest applause is from the Lord. Had He not instilled the idea that "our" money is not "ours" long before children arrived, they could not easily witness it being displayed. My selfish heart gets the best of me many times, and we have hard days when the kids and I struggle with giving up things I want and feel like I deserve. Just recently, I told my husband that I didn't want a bigger house, just a newer house with granite countertops and tile floors. A house that was already clean and well-made when we moved in. A house that didn't require us to live in a half-finished home, constantly requiring work. When I started complaining in this way, Michael quickly reminded me that I was focusing on the material things of this world. I may preface it with comments like "I don't want a bigger house, but..."; but in reality, I'm relaying that I want more and better than what we've been blessed with and how we're living as a result of following our call.

I Struggle WITH GIVING UP THINGS I WANT AND FEEL LIKE I DESERVE.

To be completely vulnerable, I struggle with the fact that I am working from home alongside my many other responsibilities and still don't have the "nice things" I believe I deserve. This comes out regularly in my conversations. I've found myself saying things like, "But I'm working and we *still* can't do this or buy that!" God then swiftly reminds me of His past provision, even when we've had nothing left. So I step forward in faith and encourage my kids to do the same. They love giving money away to their friends and in tithes to the church. If they have it, they rarely use it on themselves. I often find them digging through their toys and clothes to find items to sell, and then they use that money to bless others. Just a few weeks back, my son begged to use his birthday money to buy ice cream for our entire family. When we told him that he didn't need to use his gift and that we'd take care of it, he bawled his eyes out until we let him. It's really a miracle our children are growing this way. I wish I did more of that in my own life, but God uses children to remind all of us that we need to become like them to enter the Kingdom of heaven.

Just a few months ago, we sat down with a financial advisor for the first time to talk about some of our future financial life goals. I was unaware of how all of this would eventually pan out, considering where we were financially at the moment. I mean, we drive a 1996 suburban with over 200k miles on it that we bought for only $3,400 in cash. I watched my dear Michael explain to this advisor where we wanted to be anyway, with such authority from the Lord. He explained that we needed a certain amount of money when we eventually reached retirement age, not because we actually plan to retire, at least not from some type of ministry, but because we wanted to continue blessing others even without the same income. Yes, we want to take care of our own children and to offer them some money toward college or a business venture. But we also want to support others, including future pastors, in the same way. Setting up accountability with this financial advisor has enabled us to have a clear path and limit some other areas of our spending now to prepare for a full future.

One of the best decisions we made early in our marriage was to pursue Dave Ramsey's Financial Peace University program together. This enabled us to set up a strict budget for ourselves. It enabled us to provide an emergency fund for our family that we have regularly used and built back up, especially for car repairs, house repairs, or any other unexpected expenses. If you have not had the opportunity to be a part of one of his courses, I emphatically encourage you to sign up. I can promise you that, if you heed its guidance, it will change your life.

Marriage and Money Matters

This financial approach isn't easy and never will be. The whole idea of putting your money where your mouth is recognizes that it is all about Jesus. Your money is not truly yours, it is a gift from a gracious, good Father who loves to give good gifts to His children. This is especially true when His children view money the way He intended, as a gift that's worth giving over and over again.

This may be one of the hardest decisions to make for couples. It is something that involves both parties being aware of the true benefits of following God in this way. It requires both people to submit and follow through. If this approach resonates with you and you have an intense desire to make these changes in the dedication of your life to Christ, but your spouse is not on board, it may take a few conversations before you can completely change this dynamic within your family. Do not become bitter against your spouse or shut them out. The best approach you can take is by sitting down together while you share your heart about this matter. Make a list of some areas you can begin to change now. Even if it's not a complete revamp of your finances, it's a start on a new journey of recognizing how you can use your money to advance the Kingdom.

If, after that, your spouse is still not on board, there are little changes that you can personally make when it comes to how you would generally spend money and, instead, using it to bless others. In the meantime, pray for the softening of your spouse's heart. Again, this all comes back to perspective and viewing each and every decision through the filter of an eternal investment. This motive is the only way to live our lives with purpose, even though it can be one of the toughest facets of your life to sacrifice for the Kingdom.

Chase Your Faith:

After reading this chapter, what are the three major changes you can make to use your income to further the Kingdom of God?

How can you overcome the idea that "your" money is ultimately God's money?

CHAPTER ELEVEN

Prepared Heroes Move the World

> *"God is preparing His heroes. And when the opportunity comes, He can fit them into their places in a moment. And the world will wonder where they came from."*
> —A. B. Simpson

THROUGHOUT MY LIFE, I HAVE witnessed miracles the church works in the lives of individuals. But the most beautiful, inspiring stories are of those who have defied statistics and changed their lives. One such individual is now an incredible woman of God who came to our church as a young, single mother. She didn't know the father of her baby and she didn't have a community of support around her. Statistically, this woman should have fallen through the cracks, but she didn't. She found a family of believers, including godly men for her young son to learn from and admire. She doesn't just attend church, but she *is* the church. She loves the church and is loved by the church. I can vividly remember the first time she sat on our back porch with our church planting team in the summer of 2014 as we planned and prepared our preview services. Since then, she's been saved and baptized, and her son has been dedicated to the Lord. She serves twice a month in our kids' ministry, and she's a devoted part of one of our Life Groups. Within the community of the church, she is a hero, being prepared by the Lord to move the world. Another set of heroes within this story is a dear couple who befriended this woman and took her into their family as one of their own. They extended the invitation to her to join them in church and, through that, and their influence, she began her relationship with her Savior. This couple moved to Montana from Georgia a few years ago and has endured a great deal in the time since they've said yes to this specific call of God on their lives. The struggles they have dealt with have been incredible, resulting in the eventual death of the husband. However, the wife shared: "We said yes to God and, although it's been a hard road in doing so, we'd do it again and again over and over again, despite all the pain." These are the people who are changing the world and showing the love of the church. The people who are willing to be

> IT'S THROUGH
> *Faithfulness*
> THAT WE INCREASE OUR CAPACITY.

faithful in the little and, often unseen tasks, that God asks of them. It's through faithfulness that we increase our capacity.

Don't Be a Lone Ranger

Oh the church, what a beautiful, God-ordained blessing of community in a world full of individuals! The purpose of the church is to live in community with each other, to learn and grow as disciples, and to serve the world together. It is all about making disciples who continue to make disciples to grow the Kingdom of God. This means that working out your faith journey within the actual church should be one of your top priorities as a believer and champion of faith. We live in a world that has become more and more focused on the individual. This is a difficult topic for me to address as a pastor's wife and, as such, I am automatically viewed as someone "forcing" church upon those I love because it's important to me. But in reality, the vitality of this topic is one that cannot be discounted. In *The Purpose Driven Church* by Rick Warren, he shares that many American Christians are "floating believers."

"Anywhere else in the world, being a believer is synonymous with being connected to a local body of believers—you rarely find a lone-ranger Christian in other countries. Many American Christians, however, hop from one church to another without any identity, accountability, or commitment." [15]

This is a tragedy, and one I've seen perpetuated more and more in our society. There is great value in digging your heels in, sticking with your church, and being spurred onward by your family of believers.

There is great value in Digging Your Heels In.

The purpose of the Great Commission was spoken to the disciples prior to the start of the early church:

"Therefore go and make disciples of all nations, baptizing them in the name of the Father and of the Son and of the Holy Spirit, and teaching them to obey everything I have commanded you. And surely I am with you always, to the very end of the age." (Matthew 28:19-20).

This really speaks to the core reasons we are on this earth and what God calls us to do. This explains how the church specifically relates to this mission. God calls us to be a major influence in the world. We are meant to represent Jesus. He calls us to be a part of a purpose beyond ourselves. This can and will be accomplished beyond the walls of the church, but the church was originally designed to do these specific things as a community of believers. What provides a more profound influence on the world than people working together to make disciples? Second Timothy 4:2 tells us to "Preach the word; be prepared in season and out of season; correct, rebuke and encourage—with great patience and careful instruction."

A Body of Believers

The word "body" in reference to the church is difficult to describe, even if you're a lifelong, experienced Christian. Being a part of the body means unwrapping the gifts God has given to you specifically and using them for a greater purpose. Each of us were designed to do something in service of the church in a way that supports the rest of the church community, or body. This enables us to serve together to reach the lost.

It is not just the church body and the lost who are benefitting from your service to the church. *You* benefit. I often struggle with feeling like a slave when it comes to serving the church, as it is generally the 20% who serve the other 80%. And I have found that to be pretty accurate. But I know...

that I know...

that I know...

that God has called me to this very specific purpose. I benefit by experiencing deep fellowship and love from those I serve alongside. My spirit is filled with purpose on this earth. Most importantly, I benefit from seeing people come alive and, in turn, realizing why they were created!

Let's talk about your local church and how you were designed to fit in in a very real and tangible way. Yes, in a healthy church, you will experience deep friendship and real accountability, but this will only happen if you do your part. Rick Warren shares in *The Purpose Driven Church*, "John tells us that the proof that we are walking in the light is that we have "fellowship with one another" (1 John 1:7). If you're not having a regular fellowship with other believers you should seriously question whether or not you are really walking in the light."[16]

You can do life with those who spur you on toward greatness, but you must be where they are. Where do they spend their time? How can you be where they are to do life with them? Let's not be lukewarm believers, waiting around for others to come and serve us. Let's make real strides toward genuineness in our church community, which in turn overflows into the world. This is the real way to beat the devil, by being Christians who build each other up by doing life together. Charles Spurgeon once said: *"I do not think the devil cares how many churches you build, if only you have lukewarm preachers and people in them."*[17]

> LET'S MAKE REAL STRIDES TOWARD *Genuineness* IN OUR CHURCH COMMUNITY.

Searching for Your Strengths

We must determine our service and purpose within the church. My husband always explains, "Did I know I was good at basketball before I tried it? No, I had to practice and be around those who played, and play myself before I knew."

Often, you won't know the specific ministry God has in mind for you before you try a variety. Think you would hate working with children, the elderly, in sound, or in hospitality? Give it a shot anyway. Another important step is to take a few spiritual gifts inventories to better help you determine how your unique gifts can play into an area of ministry. After taking these inventories, give them to your pastor or a staff member and allow them to talk through the findings with you. Together, think about how they can be used in a ministry within your local church.

It's wise to take several tests. Be sure to check out the endnotes of this book for a full list of some favorites! Additionally, check out the Lifeway Spiritual Gifts Inventory included in the back of the book.

Another great tool to use in determining your area of ministry is found in the study guide for the *What On Earth Am I Here For?* study by Rick Warren. His SHAPE profile stands for Spiritual Gifts, Heart (this includes what you're passionate about), Abilities, Personality, and Experiences (includes all life experiences, both good and bad). I highly suggest that you take the opportunity to determine your SHAPE for ministry.

One important aspect to consider when it comes to living out your faith within the local church is to identify the specific goals of *your* church, and to make those your goals. Those who miss out on the beautiful blessings that come with being a member of the local church often do so because they fail to make the church *their* church. They do not identify with all that the church is and does and who God has designed them to be within the church. When Christians come together for common goals and causes, unbelievers watch in amazement. In our world today, a place filled with so much hate and sorrow, I've watched countless lost lives come to salvation in Jesus. This happens purely by watching the church be what the church is when its congregation unites and serves with a clear, common purpose in mind. It's fascinating to watch each small part of the body do its job to help make that happen.

A dear friend once told me about a time when her father had cancer. His parents were not believers and hadn't wanted anything to do with Jesus or church at any point in their lives.

However, this friend's father's church came together with the common goal of loving on and providing for him and his wife, while taking care of all the needs they had apart from treatment. His parents witnessed this incredible blessing and came to a saving relationship with Jesus. *This* is what the church is about. It's about loving and caring for each other and showing the world *why* we do it.

As a ministry wife, I tread carefully yet again when discussing the following point, but it is one that must be addressed. As a part of a local congregation, another way to show that you are a follower of your faith is to support your pastor, staff, and other ministry leaders. Encourage them, respect them, love them, care for them, and give grace upon grace. As someone who has been a witness to the behind-the-scenes aspects of running a church, I am so surprised to realize what church leaders truly give up to serve. I didn't grow up as a pastor's daughter, and I hate that I didn't know until now all they do to serve in this way. I beg you to *show* your faith by choosing to deeply love and cherish those people God has placed in leadership roles.

I want to leave you with a word of encouragement here. The church is a place for believers to come together to serve and care for others, but most importantly, to love each other while walking the narrow path. The devil will attack the unity of the church body. Don't let him win. Suffer together and lift one another up to be all that you can be for the Lord. Leave jealousy, anger, and hatred outside of the church and work toward loving, growing with, and discipling each other. This causes a ripple of change throughout our world.

Chase Your Faith:

What are three specific ways you can live out your faith within your local church starting this week?

PREPARED HEROES MOVE THE WORLD

What are some ways that you can protect the unity of the church and specifically love on those within your church?

CHAPTER TWELVE

Cause the Ripple

> *"I alone cannot change the world, but I can cast a stone across the waters to create many ripples."*
> —Mother Teresa

EXCITEMENT AROSE FOR MICHAEL AND me as we arrived at our alma mater for our final Homecoming weekend prior to moving to Montana. There were so many new changes taking place in the coming days and, finding a place of comfort with people we knew and loved, at the place where we started our life together, made all the difference for our restless minds. As we approached the welcome booth, we glanced around for familiar faces and joined in conversation with many old friends. The woman at the check-in table asked for our address. Michael gave her our current address, but added a very enthusiastic, "But just for a few days before we move to Montana!"

Another young man sitting at the welcome table responded, saying he wished he was moving to Montana. Of course, my always-believing-the-seemingly-impossible husband invited him to join our church plant in Montana. The very next night, we met this man and his sweet wife for dinner, just two days before our move. This brave couple would eventually become our source of strength. They have been vital leaders in the creation and orchestration of Bedrock Church, changing lives in our city and in the entire nation. They were willing to continue the ripple effect that God had begun in our hearts and extended to them. This eventually inspired many more to come be a part of something far bigger than themselves.

The Willing

In the book *Believing God – Day by Day*, Beth Moore declares the clear purpose God has for anyone willing, and not simply those who are gifted. She starts by sharing Luke 9:23, "He said to them all, "If anyone wants to come with Me, he must deny himself, take up his cross daily, and follow Me."

She goes on, "Two parts of a compound word leap from this verse from the Gospel of Luke: any and one. The first part—any—speaks to me about Christ's ready willingness to lead whoever will follow. We don't have to be particularly gifted, educated, or experienced. The second half—one—reminds me that Christ still extends His invitation to individuals. In ways our finite minds can hardly comprehend, Christ died for millions of ones. Yes, One died for all, but all come as one. Though His sacrifice was made for the many, our relationship with Him is one that is intensely personal."[18]

At this point in the book, you should have followed through on this process for yourself in some faith step, whether large or small. For you, it could be something big like making a major job change, moving, pursuing a different major in school, attending an entirely different school, or assuming a major ministry role. Or it could be a faith step that was smaller, but still significant, like saying "no" to some activities that were taking the place of God, giving more of your money above and beyond your tithe, or becoming more invested in the ministry of your local church. The beautiful, indescribable beauty of this is that it does not stop after the first step is taken, but rather it continues in a fluid motion for all your life. Once you've set faith as the priority in your life over your comfort, you can pursue this life of complete freedom, relishing in the One who made you and loves you.

Be aware that freedom isn't always easy. You may be free from selfishness or some of the worries of the world, but you will still wrestle with hurt and pain because we *do* live in a fallen world.

So Much Force in Such a Small Stone

The purpose of this chapter is to help you set yourself up to be the primary ripple in someone else's life as they are guided to do the same. When you start living out God's call rather than putting yourself at the forefront, people will notice. People notice God doing big things through you. You will have influence in your world. The ripple effect is the action that takes place when one of your actions influences another, who then influences another, and your entire community is changed for the cause of Christ. As a follower of your faith, how can you take a step that will cause another to take one? Throughout my life, I often don't realize the influence I have until days, weeks, or even years after an encounter with someone. This has meant an opportunity wasted to be a light for someone for some time. Since this revelation, I've learned a few things about ways to share what God has done in my life.

First of all, talk about it. In order to share what God has done in our lives, we have to actually talk about it. But how is this done, and what is the best way? For me, faith can easily be incorporated into every conversation since we moved here to follow the call. But what about the small, private things you've changed in your life? Think about what you

> IN ORDER TO SHARE WHAT GOD HAS DONE IN OUR LIVES, WE HAVE TO ACTUALLY *Talk about It.*

do and who you encounter on a daily basis. Think about what you normally talk about. Does it give life? Does it offer the hope for purpose in someone's life? This can be a beautiful catalyst for sharing the Gospel with someone who hasn't received Jesus yet. It also offers the chance for a Christian to step up to the plate and truly begin living for Jesus. When you think about it with this mindset, you can't help but talk about it without reservation. Guide it into your conversation. Make it exciting. Own it. Exclaim it, "Let me tell you about this way God has moved in my life and how I'm following through!"

Another way to share, especially in our culture today, is through social media. I find that friends from all over the world are very interested in hearing why we take these "risks" to follow God and how we're doing it. I can't speak with each of them personally, but sharing pieces of our story over my social media accounts has sparked a fire in some dear friends who have reached out to talk about their journey more.

You must remember to define how you followed through on your call. Once you heard the call and took that first step, how did you and your family continue to follow? Don't forget to talk about the hard days. We all like to have a glimpse of the struggles so we know what to anticipate. Following Jesus is not pain-free, but it's also important to talk about how great it is to follow through and how that far overshadows any pain you experience. Joy always trumps suffering. And while you may be the influencer in your circle, remember to give credit where it is due. Shining a light on yourself or your family will only go so far, but giving God credit will allow Him to impact your life and influence even more. After all, it is His journey for you, and He is working out the details.

Joy ALWAYS TRUMPS SUFFERING.

I often view myself as a meek sheep that others take advantage of because I have always given of myself over and over again until I feel I cannot give anymore. I've struggled with feeling defeated in this area because, at times, I've loved hard and have not received the same love in return. As a teenager, I used to shout, "I'm not a doormat that people can walk all over!". As an adult, I often want to scream this again, but God catches me each time and asks, "Who are you serving?" Who do I truly care about? A God who has mercifully loved me despite my hardened heart and my inability to return the same type of love to Him? Or my desire to please and plead with others to give me the unquenchable, unconditional love that I can only receive from a good, good Father. No matter what the circumstances of your life are, when you've followed through on a call from Jesus, you are a lion who roars loudly for Jesus in your sphere of influence. Don't let anyone tell you differently. People may still treat you poorly, but you are being used by the Creator to cause the roar of thunder in your world.

Remember, you set the tone for your world. Don't let people in your community silence your story or tell you it doesn't hold value. Don't let them tell you what you're doing doesn't matter, whether through their words or their actions. God is the one causing the thunder through you.

You Set the Tone **FOR YOUR WORLD.**

The way that you can continue to spread the Gospel and share your faith story is by extending your sphere of influence. Do this in two simple ways:

- ❏ Teach it to peers
- ❏ Teach it to the next generation

A Legacy

Some of the ways I accomplish teaching these two types of people in my life is by inspiring purpose in at least three other people on a regular basis. These are people who fit into one of these two categories. How does this look for me?

To inspire purpose is to give another person a reason to follow through in their faith journey. It gives them meaning, a goal, and a reason to fight hard. I do this by contacting one or two peers and one or two people in the next generation every month. I simply share my story and ask them what God is calling them to do. This allows you to continue being challenged by what God is asking *you* to do while creating a community of faith-filled people. This seems to be a bit of a phenomenon in our world today, but this is *exactly* how the disciples lived their lives. They lived in constant community, inspiring one another toward greater purpose, greater challenges, and more faithful lives.

TO INSPIRE PURPOSE IS TO GIVE ANOTHER PERSON *A Reason to Follow through.*

Another way to cause the ripple is to be a mentor for someone. Inspiring purpose and being an actual mentor require two different types of effort. Being a mentor means being devoted to the life of your mentee. It means doing whatever it takes to guide that person along the narrow path. It means actively creating a path for another to accomplish their BHAG (Big Hairy Audacious Goal). To become the mentor you need to be for someone might mean that *you* have to actually seek *them* out. Most people won't ask because they're nervous or because they won't humble themselves to ask. Just get in their lives, meet with them, develop the relationship into a mentor/mentee one that is striving toward the greater purpose of drawing closer to the Savior and taking greater risks for Him.

You're Not Doing this Alone

Often, your sphere of influence and community, in general, will feel like a wilderness. A dry desert place that is lost to the God-given passion you have. I often wonder how frequently the disciples also felt this way following Jesus' death. They lived in a world that once held the Savior, but was now completely devoid of Him. They held on to the passion of knowing Jesus personally and sharing Him with a world who had never known Him at all, or at least not on the intimate level they did. Remember this as you become a voice in the wilderness of your world. I'm preaching to myself when I say this, because frustration can easily take center stage. This is especially true when dealing with those who don't know the intimacy and beauty that comes from taking the plunge on a faith journey.

You have to adopt a missionary mindset and learn to value the hardships. And boy, do they come! As we talked about before, the devil fights hard because you are not only following your faith journey, but you're sharing it. You are inspiring others to do the same. In doing so, you will have a target on your back, your family, or whatever the devil thinks he can sink his teeth into. Don't let this scare you. Let it empower you to fight harder, roar louder, give more, and plunge deeper than you ever thought possible.

While valuing the hardships, remember to guard your heart. This year, while going through some very difficult circumstances, I joined a Bible study where we read Steven Furtick's *Crash the Chatterbox*, a book I mentioned earlier. Oh, dear one of faith, I encourage you to read through this book with at least one friend or, ideally, a community of friends of faith. It will open up your mind to the very specific battles the devil wages in your mind every single day, many of which I have fallen prey to daily. As I said earlier, the devil is a condemner and an accuser. If he can keep you accused, he can keep you unused. But clinging to the Holy Spirit as counselor keeps my head in the game. However, keeping your mind focused on Christ in the middle of a very real spiritual battle for your soul is far easier said than done. It becomes much easier to bear when you have spiritual leaders in your life rallying for you through their prayers, their words, their actions, their writings, and their love.

As You Are Going

My husband regularly uses the phrase "as you are going" when referring to the command of God to "go" in the Great Commission. The term "go" used in this verse actually means "as you are going." It is a direct call to make disciples as we are going about our daily lives. God can do a far greater thing in your life than you can even imagine. He can use you to be the influence of change in your community and to reach the exact people He has planned for you to reach. Remember that this life is not your own, but that you have a divine purpose and calling. You can be used to bring a generation of followers to Jesus. So, as you are going, continue to cause the ripple that guides people to recognize the hand of God in your life and in everything you say and do.

You Can Be Used TO BRING A GENERATION OF FOLLOWERS TO JESUS.

Chase Your Faith:

What are some specific ways you can share your faith story with your peers?

What are some specific ways you can share your faith story with the next generation?

How can you be a mentor for someone starting this week?

EPILOGUE

DRIPPING WITH SWEAT AND BREATHING heavily, my hands shaking, I stepped onto the stage at the youth girls' retreat to share my story of beauty from ashes. At twenty-three years old, it was a bold story about my earlier life as a believer in Jesus who was so unwilling to live out my calling. Fear gripped my heart as I was about to share the most intimate details of the struggles I faced and failures I endured when I was their age. It's one thing to share the testimony of the incredible miracles God has performed in your life. It's quite another to share about your failures beforehand that led to even bigger faith in a great God.

As a teenager, I found my confidence not in the God who made me, but in the value I received from friends and the attention I received from guys. I made poor choices in my desire to impress. I spent my days trying to fit in and placed my worth on how interesting I was to others. I feared fully living out my faith because of all that I would have to give up. I was left feeling powerless, alone, and unaware of what my future held.

As I shared my story with this group of girls, I held nothing back. I'm glad I didn't. After the retreat, I was then blessed to hear over and over again how my story had changed the lives of these young women. God gives us power to *literally* change lives when we are obedient to each task He gives us.

Spirit of Power

Always keep moving forward. Keep being a visionary. Dream even bigger dreams. Keep reading. Continue seeking mentors. Keep asking questions. Remember that God gives more tasks to those already doing. You will be tempted to fear this challenge, as I often have, wondering how you could possibly handle one more task, heartache, or fiery dart from the devil. But with God, you will be able to face it with less fear. 2 Timothy 1:7 reminds us, "For He has not given us a spirit of fear, but of power and of love and of a sound mind."

POWER.

He has given us power to overcome anything hindering us and anything that gets in the way of our mission and purpose. Fear is a part of the chatter that enters our minds as a direct result of the war the devil is waging over our souls. Not only does God give us absolute power, but He gives us the ability to love and to continue to love even when that seems to be a foreign concept in

EPILOGUE

our world today. So we continue to love the lost. We love those who do not have the hope of eternity apart from our passing on the Gospel. Love for the least of these. Love for our families and for the next generation. Love for all.

And along with power and love, He has given us a sound mind. A sound mind possesses the ability to squash debilitating thoughts from the devil in order to become a person capable of fulfilling all that God has called you to do.

Be a world changer, unafraid of the circumstances surrounding you, with only one healthy, holy fear of a good, loving, and gracious Father who is guiding you with His righteous hand and leading you into everlasting glory.

FAITH CHASERS,

Let's Do This.

ACKNOWLEDGMENTS

THERE ARE MANY INCREDIBLE PEOPLE who have been a part of my life and my faith journey who have enabled and inspired the content within this book. My dear husband, the last 10 years I have been so honored to call you mine. You have encouraged me, grown with me, been faithful to me, loved me beyond words, and uplifted me when we've experienced hard days. I can say that I would not have grown in my faith the way I have if not for your incredible influence and the opportunities you gave us as a couple and as a family to grow in this area. You are my biggest supporter and I love you deeply!

To my children, the ways in which you have grown and flourished in the midst of this faith journey our family has been on is incredible. I can't wait to see where God takes you in the future and I pray for your hearts to seek Him and love him. You are the future world changers! I love you so much. Be might for the Lord's army and chase the roar!

My parents, you've always believed that I could accomplish every task I set my mind to. I've never doubted your desire to see me succeed and your determination to provide me with all I needed to do that. Thank you also for displaying hard work ethic and teaching me about faith from such a young age. I love you and am so grateful for you.

My in-laws, I am so thankful that you have raised the man that is my partner for life. It is evident that you have invested in him to bring him up to be the encourager and strong man of God that he is. Thank you for loving me and welcoming me into your family with so much love. Love you!

My dear friends, the constant support I receive from you inspires me to keep going and keep pursuing! I love each of you and am so grateful for you!

Bedrock Church, thank you for being a major part of our faith journey as individuals, as a couple, and as a family. We are so glad to serve you with everything that God has given us. Thank you for loving us!

My dear mentors, without you to look up to and learn and grow from, I would not have seen the miracles of God the way I have. Thank you for encouraging and believing in me!

Colleagues, college professors, my editor, and the Self-Publishing School—thank you for making this big goal possible and for your insight, advice, and knowledge along the way!

And most importantly, my Lord and Savior. You took me out of the pit of death and changed my mourning into dancing! Thank you for being a good, good Father. Without You, I would be nothing.

NOTES

Chapter 3: A Giant Leap

1. Sarah Young, *Jesus Calling: Enjoying Peace in His Presence* (Thomas Nelson, 2004)

Chapter 5: Plankton and the Ocean Current

2. Sadie Robertson speaking at Passion City College Night

Chapter 6: Chase the Roar

3. *Webster's New World College Dictionary*, http://websters.yourdictionary.com

Chapter 7: All Your Might

4. "Great is Thy Faithfulness," http://gaither.com/news/"great-thy-faithfulness"-story-behind-hymn

5. Thom Ranier Statistic, https://www.churchcentral.com/news/survey-finds-

many-unchurched-would-come-to-church-if-invited-2/

Chapter 8: Big Faith, Bigger God

    6. Brittany's Story, http://brittanyprice.com

    7. *Life Journal*, http://www.liferesources.cc/journaling/

    8. Steven Furtick, *Crash the Chatterbox* (Multnomah, 2015)

    9. Rick Warren, *Purpose Driven Church: Every Church is Big in God's Eyes* (Zondervan, Reprint edition, 1995)

Chapter 9: Lions for Jesus

    10. Nazarene Church Growth Research

    11. LifeWay Research Data

Chapter 10: Put Your Money Where Your Mouth Is

    12. Relevant Magazine, https://relevantmagazine.com/god/church/what-would-happen-if-church-tithed

    13. Rick Warren at the 2013 Resurgence Conference

    14. Rick Warren at the 2013 Resurgence Conference

NOTES

Chapter 11: Prepared Heroes Move the World

    15. Rick Warren, *Purpose Driven Church: Every Church is Big in God's Eyes* (Zondervan, Reprint edition, 1995)

    16. *Purpose Driven Church: Every Church is Big in God's Eyes*

    17. Charles Spurgeon

    18. SHAPE, http://pastorrick.com/series/shaped-to-make-a-difference

Chapter 12: Cause the Ripple

    19. Beth Moore, *Believing God – Day by Day: Growing Your Faith All Day Long,* (B&H Books, 2008).

Online Spiritual Gifts Inventories

    http://giftstest.com/test

    http://buildingchurch.net/g2s-i.htm

    https://spiritualgiftstest.com/spiritual-gifts-test-adult-version/

SPIRITUAL GIFTS SURVEY

Copyright 2003 LifeWay Christian Resources. Reprinted and used by permission. Lifeway.com

DIRECTIONS

This is not a test, so there are no wrong answers. The ***Spiritual Gifts Survey*** consists of 80 statements. Some items reflect concrete actions; other items are descriptive traits; and still others are statements of belief.

- Select the one response you feel best characterizes yourself and place that number in the blank provided. Record your answer in the blank beside each item.

- Do not spend too much time on any one item. Remember, it is not a test. Usually your immediate response is best.

- Please give an answer for each item. Do not skip any items.

- Do not ask others how they are answering or how they think you should answer.

- Work at your own pace.

Your response choices are:

> **5**—Highly characteristic of me/definitely true for me
>
> **4**—Most of the time this would describe me/be true for me
>
> **3**—Frequently characteristic of me/true for me–about 50 percent of the time
>
> **2**—Occasionally characteristic of me/true for me–about 25 percent of the time
>
> **1**—Not at all characteristic of me/definitely untrue for me

---

1. I have the ability to organize ideas, resources, time, and people effectively.

2. I am willing to study and prepare for the task of teaching.

3. I am able to relate the truths of God to specific situations.

4. I have a God-given ability to help others grow in their faith.

5. I possess a special ability to communicate the truth of salvation.

6. I have the ability to make critical decisions when necessary.

7. I am sensitive to the hurts of people.

8. I experience joy in meeting needs through sharing possessions.

9. I enjoy studying.

SPIRITUAL GIFTS SURVEY

10. I have delivered God's message of warning and judgment.

11. I am able to sense the true motivation of persons and movements.

12. I have a special ability to trust God in difficult situations.

13. I have a strong desire to contribute to the establishment of new churches.

14. I take action to meet physical and practical needs rather than merely talking about or planning to help.

15. I enjoy entertaining guests in my home.

16. I can adapt my guidance to fit the maturity of those working with me.

17. I can delegate and assign meaningful work.

18. I have an ability and desire to teach.

19. I am usually able to analyze a situation correctly.

20. I have a natural tendency to encourage others.

21. I am willing to take the initiative in helping other Christians grow in their faith.

22. I have an acute awareness of the emotions of other people, such as loneliness, pain, fear, and anger.

23. I am a cheerful giver.

24. I spend time digging into facts.

25. I feel that I have a message from God to deliver to others.

26. I can recognize when a person is genuine/honest.

27. I am a person of vision (a clear mental portrait of a preferable future given by God). I am able to communicate vision in such a way that others commit to making the vision a reality.

28. I am willing to yield to God's will rather than question and waver.

29. I would like to be more active in getting the gospel to people in other lands.

30. It makes me happy to do things for people in need.

31. I am successful in getting a group to do its work joyfully.

32. I am able to make strangers feel at ease.

33. I have the ability to plan learning approaches.

34. I can identify those who need encouragement.

35. I have trained Christians to be more obedient disciples of Christ.

36. I am willing to do whatever it takes to see others come to Christ.

37. I am attracted to people who are hurting.

38. I am a generous giver.

39. I am able to discover new truths.

40. I have spiritual insights from Scripture concerning issues and people that compel me speak out.

41. I can sense when a person is acting in accord with God's will.

42. I can trust in God even when things look dark.

SPIRITUAL GIFTS SURVEY

43. I can determine where God wants a group to go and help it get there.

44. I have a strong desire to take the gospel to places where it has never been heard.

45. I enjoy reaching out to new people in my church and community.

46. I am sensitive to the needs of people.

47. I have been able to make effective and efficient plans for accomplishing the goals of a group.

48. I often am consulted when fellow Christians are struggling to make difficult decisions.

49. I think about how I can comfort and encourage others in my congregation.

50. I am able to give spiritual direction to others.

51. I am able to present the gospel to lost persons in such a way that they accept the Lord and His salvation.

52. I possess an unusual capacity to understand the feelings of those in distress.

53. I have a strong sense of stewardship based on the recognition that God owns all things.

54. I have delivered to other persons messages that have come directly from God.

55. I can sense when a person is acting under God's leadership.

56. I try to be in God's will continually and be available for His use.

57. I feel that I should take the gospel to people who have different beliefs from me.

58. I have an acute awareness of the physical needs of others.

59. I am skilled in setting forth positive and precise steps of action.

60. I like to meet visitors at church and make them feel welcome.

61. I explain Scripture in such a way that others understand it.

62. I can usually see spiritual solutions to problems.

63. I welcome opportunities to help people who need comfort, consolation, encouragement, and counseling.

64. I feel at ease in sharing Christ with nonbelievers.

65. I can influence others to perform to their highest God-given potential.

66. I recognize the signs of stress and distress in others.

67. I desire to give generously and unpretentiously to worthwhile projects and ministries.

68. I can organize facts into meaningful relationships.

69. God gives me messages to deliver to His people.

70. I am able to sense whether people are being honest when they tell of their religious experiences.

71. I enjoy presenting the gospel to persons of other cultures and backgrounds.

72. I enjoy doing little things that help people.

73. I can give a clear, uncomplicated presentation.

SPIRITUAL GIFTS SURVEY

74. I have been able to apply biblical truth to the specific needs of my church.

75. God has used me to encourage others to live Christlike lives.

76. I have sensed the need to help other people become more effective in their ministries.

77. I like to talk about Jesus to those who do not know Him.

78. I have the ability to make strangers feel comfortable in my home.

79. I have a wide range of study resources and know how to secure information.

80. I feel assured that a situation will change for the glory of God even when the situation seems impossible.

SCORING YOUR SURVEY

Follow these directions to figure your score for each spiritual gift.

1. Place in each box your numerical response (1-5) to the item number which is indicated below the box.

2. For each gift, add the numbers in the boxes and put the total in the TOTAL box.

LEADERSHIP	Item 6	+ Item 16	+ Item 27	+ Item 43	+ Item 65	= TOTAL
ADMINISTRATION	Item 1	+ Item 17	+ Item 31	+ Item 47	+ Item 59	= TOTAL
TEACHING	Item 2	+ Item 18	+ Item 33	+ Item 61	+ Item 73	= TOTAL
KNOWLEDGE	Item 9	+ Item 24	+ Item 39	+ Item 68	+ Item 79	= TOTAL
WISDOM	Item 3	+ Item 19	+ Item 48	+ Item 62	+ Item 74	= TOTAL
PROPHECY	Item 10	+ Item 25	+ Item 40	+ Item 54	+ Item 69	= TOTAL
DISCERNMENT	Item 11	+ Item 26	+ Item 41	+ Item 55	+ Item 70	= TOTAL
EXHORTATION	Item 20	+ Item 34	+ Item 49	+ Item 63	+ Item 75	= TOTAL
SHEPHERDING	Item 4	+ Item 21	+ Item 35	+ Item 50	+ Item 76	= TOTAL
FAITH	Item 12	+ Item 28	+ Item 42	+ Item 56	+ Item 80	= TOTAL
EVANGELISM	Item 5	+ Item 36	+ Item 51	+ Item 64	+ Item 77	= TOTAL
APOSTLESHIP	Item 13	+ Item 29	+ Item 44	+ Item 57	+ Item 71	= TOTAL
SERVICE/HELPS	Item 14	+ Item 30	+ Item 46	+ Item 58	+ Item 72	= TOTAL
MERCY	Item 7	+ Item 22	+ Item 37	+ Item 52	+ Item 66	= TOTAL
GIVING	Item 8	+ Item 23	+ Item 38	+ Item 53	+ Item 67	= TOTAL
HOSPITALITY	Item 15	+ Item 32	+ Item 45	+ Item 60	+ Item 78	= TOTAL

GRAPHING YOUR PROFILE

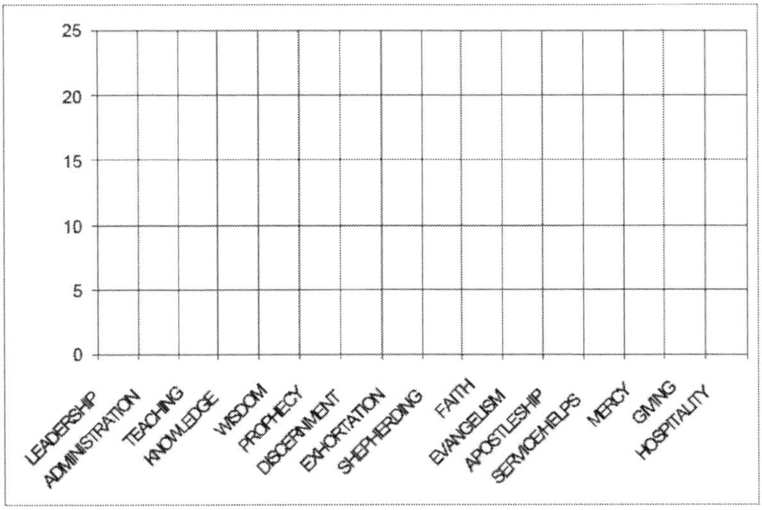
25
20
15
10
5
0
LEADERSHIP
ADMINISTRATION
TEACHING
KNOWLEDGE
WISDOM
PROPHECY
DISCERNMENT
EXHORTATION
SHEPHERDING
FAITH
EVANGELISM
APOSTLESHIP
SERVICE/HELPS
MERCY
GIVING
HOSPITALITY

1. For each gift place a mark across the bar at the point that corresponds to your TOTAL for that gift.
2. For each gift shade the bar below the mark that you have drawn.
3. The resultant graph gives a picture of your gifts. Gifts for which the bars are tall are the ones in which you appear to be strongest. Gifts for which the bars are very short are the ones in which you appear not to be strong.

CHASE THE ROAR

Now that you have completed the survey, thoughtfully answer the following questions.

The gifts I have begun to discover in my life are:

1. _____

2. _____

3. _____

- ❑ After prayer and worship, I am beginning to sense that God wants me to use my spiritual gifts to serve Christ's body by _____.

- ❑ I am not sure yet how God wants me to use my gifts to serve others. But I am committed to prayer and worship, seeking wisdom and opportunities to use the gifts I have received from God.

Ask God to help you know how He has gifted you for service and how you can begin to use this gift in ministry to others.

Copyright 2003 LifeWay Christian Resources.
Reprinted and used by permission. Lifeway.com

THE FAITH CHALLENGE

- ❏ Pray and ask God to help you determine your faith step and then continue praying about that specific step at least once a day.

- ❏ Read Scripture related to the step.

- ❏ Find a mentor and an accountability partner.

- ❏ If married, have continual conversations with your spouse about the faith step.

- ❏ Fast at least once during the determination process.

- ❏ Never allow money to determine the decision.

- ❏ Once determined, burn the ships!

ABOUT THE AUTHOR

ARIEL TYSON IS A DAUGHTER of the King, wife to a pastor, mom to five kids in six years, Montana church planter, homeschooler, college professor, lay counselor, elementary ministry director, and writer. Before beginning her career as a professor, she served as the director of a teenage girls mentoring program and is now the Girls Rock director in her church. She has loved writing throughout her entire life and has now found a greater purpose in the craft by sharing the story of what God has called her to do.

CONNECT WITH ARIEL:

Instagram – @arielctyson
Facebook – facebook.com/authorarieltyson

SELF-PUBLISHING SCHOOL

NOW IT'S YOUR TURN

Discover the EXACT 3-step blueprint you need to become a bestselling author in 3 months.

Self-Publishing School helped me, and now I want them to help you with this FREE WEBINAR!

Even if you're busy, bad at writing, or don't know where to start, you CAN write a bestseller and build your best life.

With tools and experience across a variety niches and professions, Self-Publishing School is the only resource you need to take your book to the finish line!

DON'T WAIT

Watch this FREE WEBINAR now, and Say "YES" to becoming a bestseller:

[https://xe172.isrefer.com/go/curcust/bookbrosinc3665]

Made in the USA
Columbia, SC
02 August 2021